YES

'*Yes* asks some of the uncomfortable questions that need answering: about the limits of traditional politics, who has power and why, and the direction of the UK. Whatever your views on independence these are some of the key issues which need debating and which Foley and Ramand have made an important contribution to aiding.'

Gerry Hassan, writer and academic
Author of *Caledonian Dreaming: The Quest for a Different Scotland*

'There is a growing body of evidence to suggest that independence is Scotland's chance to break from the neoliberal consensus. This book puts forward that case in a lucid and accessible manner, and is essential reading for all of us that associate with a radical vision of an empowered, better Scotland.'

Jean Urquhart MSP

'The constitutional debate in Scotland has brought to the fore a new generation of young Scottish activists, writers and thinkers, the authors of this book among them. It is greatly encouraging for our future to hear these fresh voices and the quality and depth of the analysis they bring.'

Robin McAlpine, director, Jimmy Reid Foundation
and editor, *Scottish Left Review*

'Another Scotland is not only possible, but increasingly probable. If you don't believe that – read this book. If you want to believe it and don't know how an independent Scotland could work – read this book. If you want to be inspired – read this book.'

Bernadette Devlin McAliskey, former Irish republican MP

'The push for independence is the most powerful grassroots movement Scotland has ever seen and this book constitutes its gleaming edge. Clear, lucid, and under no illusions about either the British state or the SNP, it details where the points on the moral compass must now fall. A new, transformative path for ordinary Scots lies within these pages, if we can but trust ourselves to walk it.'

Alan Bissett, author and playwright

'This book deserves to turn the referendum campaign on its head. It convincingly makes the case that the real risks for the people of Scotland lie in continuing to be part of the UK. In the process, it exposes how the "Yes" campaign has fundamentally weakened its position by implicitly accepting that change for Scotland equals danger.'

Jim and Margaret Cuthbert, economists

'Yes is the product of a youthful, dynamic and energising movement in Scotland that has successfully filled the vacuum created by traditional party political defined debates. In bravely and boldly setting out a "radical" vision for Scotland's future, the authors provide us with an invaluable basis for challenging the norm and subsequently transforming our economic institutions to better meet the needs of all of the people and not just a select few. Anyone with an interest in shaping Scotland's future should read this book.'

Ailsa McKay, Professor of Economics, Glasgow Caledonian University

'I am delighted about the publication of *Yes: The Radical Case for Scottish Independence*. It is a vital contribution to the debate, showing what independence can bring to Scotland and how vital it can be for all of us.'

Stuart Braithwaite, Mogwai

'The independence referendum is about more than Scotland. It is a vote on British nationalism, forged by Empire. Foley and Ramand vividly argue for a new beginning and set out their vision of a radically different, independent Scotland.'

Niki Seth Smith, OpenDemocracy

'For anyone interested in humanity, social justice, equality and peace, this book is a must. It strips away the lies to reveal the truth behind the "Big Stitch Up" for which we all pay such a terrible price. Another Scotland is Possible and James Foley and Pete Ramand's book is an important contribution to the debate on how to achieve it.'

David Hayman, actor

'As incisive and accessible an account of the UK's social, economic and political decline as anyone could ask for. Voters looking for an alternative to the SNP's continuity nationalism will find it in *Yes*.'

James Maxwell, *New Statesman*

'This is the voice of a new generation who look beyond short term scaremongering and petty point-scoring to ask searching questions about the Scotland we live in today and the Scotland we could live in tomorrow. An incisive and well-researched contribution which deserves to be read widely on both sides of the independence debate – and even more so, among those who have yet to make up their minds.'

Alan McCombes, co-author of *Imagine: A Socialist Vision for the 21ˢᵗ Century*

'A bold vision of an Independent Scotland – you may not agree with everything written here, but this book is certainly a landmark on the Road to Independence: it is refreshing, radical and full of passion – everything we need to win the referendum in September 2014 (and beyond!).'

Aamer Anwar, Lawyer and Human Rights Campaigner

'Whether or not you embrace all of this book's conclusions, it brings a welcome breath of fresh thinking to a sterile debate, and reminds us that social values and justice need not go out of fashion.'

Ruth Wishart, journalist and broadcaster, former assistant editor of the *Sunday Mail, Scotsman* and *Sunday Standard*

'Non-nationalist arguments for Scottish independence have been all too rare in the current debates about the nation's future. We should be grateful then that James Foley and Pete Ramand have written a book which puts the case squarely in terms of the crisis of British capitalism, neoliberalism, and the struggle for social justice. ... This book is essential reading for everyone interested in the left-wing case for Scottish independence.'

Neil Davidson, University of Glasgow, author of *Discovering the Scottish Revolution*

YES

The Radical Case for Scottish Independence

James Foley & Pete Ramand

www.plutobooks.com

First published 2014 by Pluto Press
345 Archway Road, London N6 5AA

www.plutobooks.com

Distributed in the United States of America exclusively by
Palgrave Macmillan, a division of St. Martin's Press LLC,
175 Fifth Avenue, New York, NY 10010

British Library Cataloguing in Publication Data
A catalogue record for this book is available from the British Library

ISBN   978 0 7453 3475 2   Paperback
ISBN   978 1 7837 1132 1   PDF eBook
ISBN   978 1 7837 1134 5   Kindle eBook
ISBN   978 1 7837 1133 8   EPUB eBook

Library of Congress Cataloging in Publication Data applied for

This book is printed on paper suitable for recycling and made from fully managed
and sustained forest sources. Logging, pulping and manufacturing processes are
expected to conform to the environmental standards of the country of origin.

10   9   8   7   6   5   4   3   2   1

Typeset from disk by Stanford DTP Services, Northampton, England
Text design by Melanie Patrick
Simultaneously printed digitally by CPI Antony Rowe, Chippenham, UK
and Edwards Bros in the United States of America

For Linda and Anne

Contents

List of Figures

Acknowledgements

Two years ago, journalist David Torrance released a biography of Alex Salmond, predicting that the 2007-11 government would be his last. History thumped Torrance's forecast in the face; but we feel he deserves our sympathy. We are also writing about history on the move. We hope readers will forgive our miscalculations in this book, which was written in the eight weeks of September and October 2013. Things may change; if our predictions fail, we promise to accept our errors with good cheer.

This project would have been impossible without the support of a number of people – far too many to name. But in particular we would like to thank our parents and families, Cat Boyd, Daniel Foley and Jenna Gormal for their encouragement, guidance and patience throughout this process. We could not have completed this project without them.

Reem Abu-Hayyeh, Allan Armstrong, Gareth Beynon, Linda Croxford, Aisling Gallagher and Ben Wray provided invaluable comments on various drafts of the book. We are very grateful for their counsel.

Over the years we benefited from conversations with many people who informed our ideas and arguments. It is impossible to mention all of them in this short space. But in particular we would like to thank Chris Bambery, Sam Beaton, Willie Black, Eileen Boyle, Nik Brown, Fred Cartmel, Brian Christopher, Gregor Clunie, Sarah Collins, Megan Cowie, Sean Coyle, Neil Davidson, Lucky Dhillon, Sinead Dunn, Mohammed Elijas, James Ferns, Bridget Fowler, Adam Frew, Gerry Hassan, David Jamieson, Jayasree Kalathil, James Kennedy, Kezia Kinder, Gavin Lavery, Scott Lavery, Jamie Maxwell, Robin McAlpine, Alan McCombes, Callum McCormick, Kerri McGahey, Danny McGregor, Fiona McPhail, Jenny Morrison, Phil Neal, Liam O'Hare, Suki Sangha, Jonathon Shafi, Bryan Simpson, Pat Smith, Bohdan Starosta, Jim Taggart, Dominique Üçbaş, Chris Walsh, Raymond Watt and Liam Young. We are, of course, entirely responsible for any mistakes and errors contained in the following pages.

Jonathan Hearn and Phillip Grant at Edinburgh University allowed James Foley a break from his PhD to complete this project. We thank them for their patience.

Finally we would like to thank David Castle, our editor at Pluto Press, for his advice, comments and help throughout the process of writing this book.

Introduction

In 2007, Holyrood's Labour executive trailed Alex Salmond's SNP in the polls, and Tony Blair, already leaving Downing Street, made a fateful choice. The election, he decided, should focus on his personal honour. 'There was a feeling I shouldn't, but I was equally clear I should go [to Scotland] and put real credibility on the line,' he recalls in his memoirs.[1] Defying the two-thirds opposition to the Iraq War, he toured the country, railing against nationalism and Alex Salmond. Blair warned that independence would cost every Scottish family £5,000, an alarmist slice of fantasy arithmetic dreamed up by Whitehall officials. Despite his habit of grovelling to business leaders, he labelled SNP supporter George Mathewson, an elite Scottish banker, 'absurd' and 'self-indulgent'. His cringeworthy photo ops with Scottish voters, he later admitted, were stage-managed to avoid awkward questions. But there was no escaping Iraq.

Blair's Scottish tour was his last significant act as Labour leader, and he had cause to regret it. He felt like an 'outsider', and was 'never passionate' about devolution.[2] Besides, his very public loathing for Salmond's SNP, together with voter resentment over his alliance with George W. Bush, granted the nationalists victory; even Blair admits this. Since then, the SNP received resounding approval for a second term. 'I knew once Alex Salmond got his feet under the table, he could play off against the Westminster government and embed himself,' Blair concedes.[3] Aside from invading Iraq, his major legacy was handing Scottish nationalists an indefinite right to govern Holyrood. Just as Thatcher's policies had produced devolution, so Blair's transformation of Labour produced 2014, perhaps the biggest threat to British statehood for generations.

This bungling came on the third centenary of the Act of Union. There were few celebrations marking this founding event of modern Britain, and any commemorations were subdued. This was curious for two reasons. First, when Scotland united with England, it marked the beginning of two centuries of global domination, where Britannia truly ruled the waves, and commanded a quarter of the world's people. Value judgements aside, these events were as significant to history, by some measures, as the French Revolution or America's War of Independence. Yet they passed almost unnoticed. Secondly, Britain's rulers kept insisting, since Thatcher, that we should stop apologising for our legacy of Empire. New Labour trumpeted its patriotic credentials by draping a bulldog in a Union Jack, and toured the Commonwealth reminiscing about pith helmets and stiff upper lips. But the anniversary of the British pact met, at best, with a polite cough of acknowledgement.

Blair and Brown staked their reputations on restoring Britain to its former glory. Hence, they volunteered to speak for all global leaders on two pivotal occasions: Blair for Bush's war on terror, and Brown for bailing-out bankers in 2008. But beneath these showcases for British leadership lay fractures in the state's skeletal structure. Scotland, no longer cowed by decades of Tory rule, was asserting its independence from Labour, recoiling from three parliaments of domestic failures and foreign policy horrors.

Scotland's vote in 2014 opens subversive prospects and will decide a great deal. If Scots reject independence, Britain will get a momentary infusion of purpose, having postponed the biggest threat to the British state's existence. Combined with patriotic reveries over Royal babies and opening ceremonies and routine wars, a new conservative confidence will emerge. If Westminster can impose austerity while upholding order on the streets, Britain may see a decade of consensus, based on more of the status quo. Without question, by 2030, the UK will have among the highest inequalities in Europe, an economy dominated by arms companies and banks, and a regressive attitude towards climate change. Westminster will resemble Washington, with two (or perhaps three) authoritarian parties divorced from a low-paid majority. Britain's present path will continue: pretensions to global rule on the surface, built on a foundation of minimal workfare citizenship.

A 'Yes' vote would throw the status quo into doubt. Certain collisions, for instance housing Trident nuclear missiles – a key plank of the US's strategy in Europe – would be unavoidable. The White House and the Pentagon would no longer regard Britain as a reliable diplomatic cover, and a blow to UK prestige would force the remains of Westminster to rethink their global ambitions. All of these events would be virtuous, offering opportunities to redirect wasteful military spending to civilian purposes, and shift subsidies from arms companies to green industries. Britain's retreat from great-power politics would not harm its citizens, who have suffered for the sake of the Atlantic alliance.

Scotland's path would be less clear. By itself, voting Yes offers no guarantees of a better, more progressive future, never mind a radical redistribution of wealth and power. Scotland would face creating a new state under hostile circumstances, after decades where states have eroded expectations about national citizenship. The right to free education, universal healthcare, and support for the disabled, unemployed, and pensioners are no longer guaranteed. Not every state has gone to UK or US extremes, but most have slid backwards, withdrawing earlier post-Second World War commitments. If Scottish rulers, politicians and managers conform to consensus assumptions about national welfare, and if Scotland's people do not resist them, we could reproduce many of Britain's current problems. With minimal rights, and low wages, we could enter a 'race to the bottom' with peripheral European economies.

But creating a new state opens opportunities as well as risks. Most of Northern Europe has more progressive taxation, a better standard of living, and fairer social guarantees than Britain. They work shorter hours, they are happier, and they suffer fewer inequalities.[4] They also regard benefits such as free childcare as integral to citizenship, while Britain makes no concessions to women's unpaid labour. At minimum, Scotland could aim to copy the example of its non-British neighbours, and define a social citizenship against Britain's neoliberal citizenship. For all its faults, the Nordic model has many virtues in comparative terms. Pundits can exaggerate and romanticise differences between Britain and Scandinavia; but they have factual grounds.

A progressive case for Scottish independence would aim to mirror the best approaches to national citizenship under today's capitalism, creating a 'Nordic utopia'. To an extent, Salmond's SNP already adopt this approach. The UK, unique among European countries, has no bill of citizen rights or written constitution. Salmond has proposed that a Scottish constitution would guarantee the right to free education, outlaw homelessness, ban nuclear weapons, and set clear restrictions on armed force. The SNP conference in 2013 promised to examine the Common Weal initiative, launched by the Jimmy Reid Foundation, which aims to put Scotland on a path to Nordic citizenship. The present policy vacuum, with UK-style neoliberalism intellectually exhausted by the 2008 crisis, presents openings for left-of-centre agendas. Norway, Sweden, Denmark and the Netherlands prove that such models are workable, and few would doubt they are desirable.

Such alternatives would find no place in Westminster. The Commons is institutionally gridlocked, disenfranchising opponents of neoliberal norms. Labour, Liberals and Tories are committed to the same policies on world affairs, austerity and immigration. Scotland has a different consensus on these issues, but Holyrood has no levers to change them. Beyond Parliament, other British institutions help to enforce UK inequalities, including the City of London, the arms trade and a rotten conformism in the civil service.

But although we find the progressive case appealing, compared to Westminster, our aim here is not to defend this vision. We wish to go a step further, and define what we call a radical vision for independence, which we distinguish in three ways. First, while new contracts between states and citizens might be steps in the right direction, we should not collapse into legalist fallacies. Rights are only worth having if we can defend them. So besides written rights and pleas for 'fairness', we need to know who benefits, and how they organise through political alliances. Even when we subtract Westminster and its wars and nuclear bombs, Scotland will remain a capitalist, class-divided society. Unless we know how property behaves, our rights are token gestures, not firm guarantees of social progress.

Secondly, a radical vision goes further than the mixed economies of Northern Europe. As Robin Hahnel observes, 'the backward trajectory of social democracy in Scandinavia … stands as a reminder of why we must go beyond capitalism if we expect to sustain progress toward the economics of equitable cooperation.'[5] The Nordic examples are useful, because they prove the nonsense of Westminster's slogan, 'there is no alternative'. But like all capitalist societies, they are not equipped for the challenges of the twenty-first century, and a just, sustainable Scotland would have to go further, setting new precedents. To redress climate change and the rise of the 1 per cent, most economic decisions must be transferred out of private hands and placed under public control.

Third, radicals refuse to let Westminster set the agenda about independence. We take every opportunity to condemn the UK's redundant economic model, its grotesque inequalities and its senile militarism. The Scottish media, upholding conformist ideas of economic and political security, mangles the realities and risks of independence. No 'Yes' supporter should fear stating the obvious. Britain, in partnership with the US, leads the way in making the world unsafe; its free market system makes most of its citizens insecure. For independence activists, trying to show that Scotland can match the UK's armed forces or strong currency is a trap, and it may be avoided. Britain's assertion of armed force in Afghanistan and Iraq put millions in harm's way. Britain's commitment to appeasing bondholders and finance led to a massacre of jobs in the 1980s and now poses decades of unrelenting austerity. There are better alternatives to this scandalous waste of resources. Westminster, in other words, needs to prove it can change; but at present, many 'Yes' supporters feel compelled to show how little will change. Our national discourse is back-to-front.

The Economy

The independence debate occurs in particular circumstances, amid the biggest economic crisis since the 1930s. This context should cause us to rethink existing models of economic security. Before the crisis, the SNP argued:

> Off our east coast lies Norway, the second most prosperous country in the world. Off our west coast lies Ireland, the fourth most prosperous country in the world. Off our north coast lies Iceland, the sixth most prosperous country in the world. These independent countries represent an *arc of prosperity* – and Scotland has every bit as much potential as them.[6]

Today, the phrase 'arc of prosperity' makes a mockery of the economic case for a Yes vote. Ireland's neoliberal model is an object of pity rather than envy, and Dublin is a byword for financial incompetence. Iceland is hardly a model economy either. Unionists never tire of observing the sorry fate of independent European nations. Small countries are exposed as vulnerable and unable to compete, and nobody wants to end up like Greece. Hence, the neoliberal case for Scottish independence – small, competitive states in niche markets – will not work. Unionists insist, pointing to crumbling economies around us, that we benefit from the security of a bigger state, and 'we are better together'. United, they argue, Britain has more power to combat crises and face down the EU.

But are small economies extra vulnerable to recession? On closer inspection, this assumption seems dubious. Britain, a large and globalised economy, suffered a major crash and has continued to worsen. Five years after the banking collapse, output was still 3 per cent down, while even the sluggish US economy has grown by 5 per cent. Other big economies, for example, Spain and Italy, show the futility of measuring an economy's endurance by its size. By contrast, the economies of Denmark and Norway have weathered the crisis and Sweden has continued to grow (see Figure I.1). These countries hold their own currencies and tolerate far fewer inequalities (see Figure I.2).

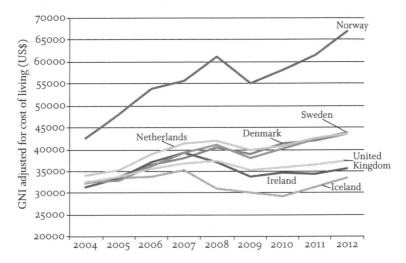

Figure I.1   UK economy vs small North European economies
Source: The World Bank

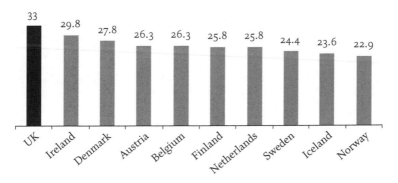

Figure I.2   Rate of income inequality (GINI): UK vs small North European economies
Source: Eurostat

Small, therefore, does not mean more vulnerable or economically weaker. Instead, to explain crises like 2008, three other variables are decisive. The countries suffering the heaviest crashes were those that clung closest to the neoliberal troika of free trade, deregulation and privatisation.

Together, these factors prompted risky lending booms, often combined with property market bubbles, creating deceptive growth in construction sectors. But so-called 'free markets' were not enough to cause the crash. Bankers and financiers only took such heavy risks because they believed governments would not let them fail. Underlying their adventurous private capitalism was simple trust in the social power and political sway of national governments. As Professor David Simpson remarks:

> Banks in countries like Iceland and Ireland had been able to run up large liabilities, because their creditors and depositors anticipated that their Governments would always bail them out in time of need. *Once Governments make it clear that in future insolvent banks will be allowed to fail, then the size of a country in relation to the liabilities of its banking system should no longer be a problem.*[7]

Hence, small economies are only more vulnerable if they conform to a UK-style neoliberalism. If Scotland promised to socialise the risks of globalised banks, while keeping profits in private hands, then it would face obvious dangers. But if bankers knew that taxpayer bailouts were conditional on conforming to democratic objectives, then a different investment strategy would result. Westminster's bailouts reflected decades of political preferences towards speculation and debt-fuelled finance. Scotland does not have to follow this model, and if banks engage in privatised gambling, beyond public scrutiny, they should face the risk of failure.

Perhaps the answer is not just 'fail', but also 'jail'. Iceland set a clear precedent by letting banks go bankrupt and putting corrupt speculators in prison. British bankers, by contrast, have continued to reward themselves massive bonuses and payoffs, and unregulated finance continues unchanged. The tiny Icelandic economy, having suffered total meltdown, will be ahead of the UK in its recovery by 2014, according to current IMF estimates.[8] Iceland, lest we forget, suffered the worst possible catastrophe of a small economy; yet once again it outperforms united Britain.

Thus, two factors explain exposure to crisis: the degree of deregulation, and bankers' faith in unqualified government support. But what about recovery from a crash like 2008? Here, the answer is simple. The more governments impose austerity, the slower they recover; those that re-inflate the economy almost always do better (see Figure I.3). Capitalism makes crises inevitable, but certain strategies work better than others, and austerity benefits bondholders and elites, not economies as a whole.

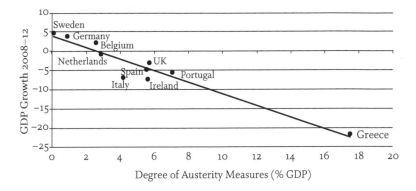

Figure I.3   Austerity shuts down growth in Europe: 2008–12

Source: World Bank Fiscal Monitor Oct 2012 and Eurostat

Returning to Scottish independence, both sides miss the essence of economic stability. Unionists say that Scotland, as a small isolated economy, would be more vulnerable than Britain. On empirical grounds, these assumptions are false: equivalent neighbouring economies combine higher living standards and greater equality. Even the worst offenders, like Iceland and Ireland, who bought into the false promises of neoliberal growth and suffered severe emergencies, will recover better than Britain. Nationalists are wrong, or were wrong, to argue that an independent Scotland can succeed by liberalising and competing on corporation tax. Correlations between an economy's size and its vulnerability are weak. The most unstable nations are those that conform to the neoliberal rulebook.

These pro-market norms, we should remember, had a specific source. The failed economic ideas of the past era made up the 'Washington Consensus', with messianic fervour pressed upon others by the US-UK alliance. Both economies saw limited real wage growth even in boom years. Instead, the benefits of the US-UK bubbles in finance and dot.com went to fund luxurious lifestyles for rich elites. As a result, investment plummeted, debt soared, and the poor suffered the brunt of recessions.

We believe Scotland has the opportunity in 2014 to break with this model. But independence offers no guarantees of radical, necessary economic change. To make sure we avoid another 2008, we must change on three fronts. First, Scotland must abandon the view that deregulation, private ownership and free trade benefit the economy. Secondly, we would need to rebalance rewards, risks and punishments. Those who take risks that harm public welfare should face jail-time, not bailouts. Third, where recessions do happen, we should end the insanity of austerity, and raise government spending to create jobs and fund investment. In the present era, this would mean a 'Green New Deal' to meet our future energy needs, with clear targets for ending poverty.

In opposition to the 'Washington Consensus', we must build a consensus against neoliberal policies in Scotland. A Yes vote would not make this appear by magic, and elite interests will risk massive upheaval to maintain their present privileges. But Scotland already possesses resources to build a better society. This, of course, comprises North Sea oil and our green energy potential, among the highest in Europe. But it also includes a left-of-centre climate of opinion, which would have far greater muscle under independence. Political will, allied to organised working people, is crucial to our future as much as oil or climate infrastructure. Scotland does not suffer from scarcities; our assets are mismanaged, and this can be corrected.

No electable Westminster party offers alternatives to neoliberal norms, even as austerity jeopardises most peoples' living standards. The big three all pander to big business, and corporate interests are embedded in UK politics more than any rival polity. All parties, moreover, are committed to purchasing massive military items, like £80 billion Trident missiles, at taxpayers' expense. And the main opposition to this comes from UKIP, which is driving Westminster politics further to the right. Westminster cannot shift leftwards by its own momentum. It would need a transformative shock, either a miraculous revolt of citizens from below or a cataclysmic world event, to turn Labour against austerity and American power.

So while independence poses risks, these should be placed in proper context. The prospect of Westminster rule means decades of manufactured uncertainty. Remaining in the UK endangers livelihoods, by forcing vulnerable people to rely on the market, as the Bedroom Tax shows, or by sacrificing our youth, at the US's behest, in illegal wars. If Scots vote No, they will secure the present insecurity.

We can have no illusions about contemporary Scotland. Instinctive collectivism may prevail in parts of society, but things are far from even. Edinburgh has a greater ratio of children in private school (20 per cent) than any other region of Britain. There are millionaire hotspots across Scotland, and the number of million-pound homes has shot up in the recession. The wealthiest Scots earn 273 (two hundred and seventy three!) times more than the poorest families.[9] This shabby order is indefensible, and independence should serve those who wish to change it. A Yes vote is more than a protest against the injustices of UK capitalism. It can be the first step towards a better society, one that sets precedents of social and environmental justice, rather than dehumanising its citizens in a race to the bottom.

Two Nationalisms

Scottish voters are judging more than Britain's economic model. The 2014 vote poses questions of identity, experience and oppression. On these matters, we are also confronted with mystifying assumptions, mirages and an overpowering conformism. In particular, a depressing feature of Scottish public dialogue has been the sterile, uncritical conceptions of 'nationalism'. In the mainstream media universe, Salmond is a nationalist, but pith-helmeted Blair and Brown are … internationalists? The *Daily Record*, to take one example, ran an editorial urging Scottish trade unionists to turn away from the siren's call of blood and soil. 'The clue is in the name – unions are about unity,' they argued. 'Nationalism, no matter how it is dressed up, is about dividing people.'[10] As a result, organised workers should vote to keep the British state, QED.

These editorials are correct in certain details. Nation states divide more than they unite; humanity deserves better than arbitrary borders separating people by so-called 'ethnic origins'. But this abstract truism adds nothing to understanding 2014. The latent premise of *Daily Record* unionism says that a No vote means a stance against nationalism. This masks alarming misconceptions about the content and dangers of nationalist ideas.

In historical terms, the most dangerous nationalisms derive from powerful states. This has dragooned young men and women from humble backgrounds to sacrifice their lives, face down in muddy fields, for the territorial ambitions of speculators, aristocrats and militarists. The true risk of these ideas concerns their routine, unacknowledged nature, what Michael Billig calls their 'banality' (see Chapter 2). By contrast, other nationalisms belong to weaker nations, and aim to arouse passionate indignation at injustice, to enfeeble stronger rivals and gain support for statehood. These latter movements are dismissed by powerful nations as pathological. Hence, ruling groups claim they are immune from nationalist temptations, which belong to simpletons and backward peoples, but their political authority rests on mobilising loyalty to the state. Clearly, Britain's dominant ideas are nationalisms of this sort, expecting citizens' instinctive and uncritical docility, while warning that rival sovereignties are toxic.

The SNP relies on two methods to create a new nation state. First, it seeks public approval for its party policies in the semi-autonomy of Holyrood. Secondly, it aims to mobilise a social movement to build a popular mandate for Scottish sovereignty. There is scant evidence that it attempts either practice in a divisive fashion, not in recent decades. There are a few ultra-fanatical fringe groups who rant against English colonists, but they are a tiny minority of nationalist opinion. Six per cent of SNP members were born in England, which more or less equates to the proportion of English people Scotland-wide.[11]

By contrast, what we call British nationalism revolves around invading and occupying other nation states. During routine Westminster wars, the media bombards the UK with divisive and racialised images, from Muslims refusing to conform to 'our' values, to immigrants arriving to steal 'our' jobs. The *Sun*, the *Daily Mail* and those other 'patriotic' outlets are never short of MPs and ministers to stoke fears of 'Others'. Pompous narratives of an aristocracy of Empire, with a right to rule the world, linger in Westminster discourse. 'Century upon century it has been the destiny of Britain to lead other nations,' intoned Tony Blair. 'That should not be a destiny that is part of our history. It should be part of our future.'[12] All displays of British public pomp and pride revolve on themes of racial superiority, blood lineage, and might-makes-right; hence, the Royal family.

By examining Scottish and British nationalism, a few contrasts should be clear. Both can involve mythologised references to traditions, national bonds and kinship. Therefore, both nationalisms fuse reactionary and progressive elements to move their people into action. In 1995, Alex Salmond hailed the SNP Conference, 'with Wallace – head and heart – the one word that encapsulates all our hopes – freedom, freedom, freedom!'[13] British nationalism, forged by Empire, places different emphases and aspires to more than mere nationhood. UK rulers are unhappy at being an equal nation with Denmark, Poland, or Canada; they wish to comport themselves as a Civilisation. They are burdened with a legacy of mastering other nations, bringing them the splendiferous benefits of Enlightenment, Christianity and free trade.

Britain cannot aspire to dominance today, but this reinforces the nationalist element, as we will outline. For policy makers, reasserting Britain on the world stage, by allying with the US, remains an overarching goal. Grass-roots British nationalism seeks to protect the privileges of a dominant race from immigration: 'British jobs for British workers'. Every major party in Westminster flirts with this brand of rhetoric. Gordon Brown coined the phrase, after all, and trade union leaders from Unite adopted it before Nick Griffin gave it a permanent home. Holyrood politics avoids racial competition in elections, to the credit of all parties.

Both Scottish and British nationalism use mythology and appeals to tradition to gain consent and to steer voters' political aspirations. But are the desires of social movements for autonomy more divisive than the desire of powerful states to enhance their influence by violent force? Some Scots might feel excluded or alienated by a Yes vote. But what if Labour or Tories, appealing to superior British values and asserting our right to police other nations, invades another Iraq or Afghanistan? This would guarantee conflict and bitterness, at home and abroad. British nationalism glorifies might and strength, aiming to whip the population into a state of readiness for conquest, often phrased as 'defence'.

While Britain is consistent, Scottish nationalism is confused with respect to Empire and race. The problem is that knowing where Britain ends and Scotland begins is very difficult. Scots played a practical role in the British Empire, as soldiers, settlers, churchmen, traders, financiers and slave owners. An 'absurdly high proportion' of Empire administrators were Scottish, notes Neal Ascherson.[14] Scots also contributed to the Empire's emotions and sentiments. And thus, today, the Scottish identity blends with nostalgia for world conquest. 'Presbyterianism and plunder', with 'an indecent share of the spoils of Empire', soldered the Scots to the Union.[15] The Church of Scotland, that most definitive institution, sprawls across the globe thanks to missionary colonialists. Often, its influence has been benign, but its toxicity should be noted: in 1923, the Kirk released a report entitled *The Menace of the Irish Race to our Scottish Nationality*.

Untangling a Scottish sense of pride from a British and Protestant sense of privilege is tortuous. Scottish identity has increased in recent decades; but its roots are often very shallow. Pre-union Scottish legends, those ancient memories of Wallace and Bruce, make little practical impact on consciousness. Like many Scots, our ancestors lived in England, Ireland, or (in the case of one of this book's authors) India at the time of the Wars of

Independence. Our emotional ties to tradition are not Scottish, and here we resemble much of Scotland.

For others, it applies the other way. Scots can sustain bonds to the distant past while supporting a practical alliance with the British state. Hence, one can, without contradiction, celebrate Bannockburn, hate England at football, and vote No in 2014. Many Scots undoubtedly will. This conclusion is backed by research, which shows that *how Scottish you feel* has little or no impact on how you will vote in 2014. Twenty-three per cent of Scots identify as Scottish and not British; 30 per cent as more Scottish than British. But this does not total 53 per cent support for independence.[16] Even those who firmly reject British identity are not guaranteed to vote Yes; far from it.

In terms of emotion, tradition and identity, the key battle for 2014 is about Britain, not Scotland. But the mainstream Yes campaign avoids the issue of the UK. Instead, it has allowed the media to frame this element of the debate. Yes campaigners are urged to concentrate on the 'positive' message, making Scots optimistic about being Scottish. We think that unless this bias is reversed, the debate will be lost. Britishness, we argue, is the missing link in the debate, and failing to discuss it limits the Yes case. 'The SNP s task is not to encourage Scots to feel more Scottish,' notes *Herald* columnist Ian Bell, 'but to persuade them to feel less British.'[17]

We are excited by the prospect of breaking up Britain. A Yes vote would close a dark chapter of Scottish history, and force all UK nations to confront our colonial past. It would end the fantasy of holding Europe down with nuclear force, rather than diplomacy. And it would weaken, beyond redemption, one of the most reactionary American client regimes in world affairs. As internationalists, we welcome these prospects, and wish to persuade others across Britain that Scottish independence is the first step towards changing our unjust society.

Outline of This Book

In Chapter 1, we define the elements of contemporary British nationalism. We look at how Britain adjusted to the loss of Empire in two phases: the period of 'decline', and the post-Thatcher period of 'renaissance'. The past few decades have seen an element of boosterism in British ideology. Especially on the economic and geopolitical front, the alliance with American capitalism gave a revived sense of historical purpose to the

English-speaking world. We borrow Niall Ferguson's term 'Anglobalisation' to describe this idea, which implies continuous purpose between UK and US Empires. We also outline four fronts where this approaches the point of crisis: economic, geopolitical, social and democratic. Scottish independence, we suggest, is in part a cumulative product of these crises.

Chapter 2 addresses directly the question of British identity and nationalism as 'missing links' in the independence debate. It examines the idea of a chauvinist element in Scottish nationalism, and looks at the realities of racist violence. We point to the Britishness of Scottish racism, showing how a false dichotomy between Scotland and Britain causes confusion.

Chapter 3 looks at changes in Scottish private capitalism. Many assume Scotland has a 'left-wing civil society', and that a 'Nordic model' of high welfare spending follows from independence. We wish to examine the barriers to this: particularly, organised business interests in Scotland that will resist any radical reforms to redistribute wealth. In recent decades, parts of Scotland have been at the vanguard of privatisation and neoliberal politics. We wish to show that, since Scottish capital will not surrender its resources voluntarily, we need an adequate account of the reproduction of private power in Scotland to define an alternative.

Chapter 4 looks at parliamentary politics in Scotland. It looks at why the Scottish Parliament is more left-wing, but also how Westminster still drags Scottish Labour to the right. We examine how New Labour scoured the party of left-wing and 'soft-nationalist' opponents to achieve total hegemony. We also examine the social basis of the SNP, claims they are left or right wing, and the tensions that will arise after 2014.

Chapter 5 argues that the strategic weaknesses in the Yes campaign must be addressed. We look at the problems in Yes Scotland, its conformist politics, and its intellectual weaknesses.

Chapter 6 develops the contours of a radical agenda for Scotland. It looks at the need for a clear sense of 'agency', that is, who is going to support radical change, and 'coercion', or how Scottish elites will organise to defend their interests. A radical agenda, we propose, must be partial, and must take sides not 'for' Scotland against Britain, but for the Scottish working class against the Scottish capitalists and landowners who shelter under the British state. We make some suggestions of what alternative forms of radical democracy may entail, as well as looking at the components of practical policies to reverse the slide towards market rule.

1

Endgame Britain? The Four Crises of 'Anglobalisation'

In the twelve months after the Yes campaign was launched, the UK lost its triple-A credit rating, finalised its humiliating withdrawal from Afghanistan, and saw 350,000 people rely on food banks to stave off hunger. But many analysts cringe at these topics, considering them impertinent to the 2014 debate. Column inches are dedicated to 'what Scotland thinks', pouring over the minutiae of voter intentions and the intrigues of party leaders. The debate's substance, the British state, often disappears in this haze.

Public opinion is crucial, but its terms are not fixed. Rather than treat voters as a passive bundle of neuroses, we should remind them of the urgency of change, addressing the citizen, not the psyche. Otherwise, by focusing on individual impulses, conservative forces will set the agenda and define the meaning of 2014.

Yes supporters tend to downplay the vote's significance, fearing it will startle potential supporters. But if we tell people they are terrified of change, they will start to believe it. If you fear the unknown, why vote for separation? Instead, we should treat citizens as rational and mature enough to handle the implications of their decision. The stakes are very high, as Scotland's vote could consign the British state to history. No referendum has ever had such far-reaching consequences. Every four years, we register views on politicians, but how often do we decide the fate of a global power?

Our analysis of independence thus begins with the ideology of Britain today. Fantasies of national destiny are common to all Westminster parties, but they receive little scrutiny. By outlining Britain's ruling ideas, we expose their 'nationalist' core. British politics relies on an imaginary sense of power and purpose; but reality often intrudes, exposing the shabbiness of Westminster's ambitions. When facts trespass on prevailing assumptions, a crisis results; and UK politics faces crises on many fronts.

Anglobalisation

Britain was the first truly capitalist nation state, and despite its gradual democratisation, its core institutions survived disruptions intact. Unlike European rivals, it escaped convulsions of invasion and revolution for over three centuries. While other states chopped off heads, swung dictators from lampposts, and restructured parliaments, the UK evolved in bits and pieces. Existing elites absorbed democratic challenges with minimal upheaval. Labour sold the welfare state as an extension of the privileges of Empire.

Although the establishment retained its privileges, this did not insulate Britain from wider events. In lieu of radical change, Britain suffered a century-long erosion of power. For most of the 1900s, Westminster contemplated 'decline', ceding influence to American and European challengers.

Two issues highlighted Britain's woes. First, after 1945, Britain surrendered its Empire, pressured from above by the US and from below by anti-colonial uprisings. Preserving a Commonwealth trading area and a Sterling zone slowed, but did not stop, this slump of global ambition. The US quashed an Anglo-French-Israeli invasion of Suez in 1956, proving Britain's shrivelling relevance. Paralysing conflicts within Britain's industries during the 1960s and 1970s heightened these problems, leading to the tag 'the sick man of Europe'. Britain had enjoyed a rapid rise to imperial power and industrial supremacy in the nineteenth century; but in a century it vanished.

Britain's elites saw waning influence overseas and workers' strength in industry as two parts of the same problem. Both symbolised decline. This is why British ideology pivots around Margaret Thatcher. Her reign, according to present-day mythology, restored national pride on both fronts. Thatcher identified a common enemy ('socialism') both at home and abroad; by declaring war on this rot, she reversed Britain's malaise and lifted the gloom.

Even critics point to Thatcher's 'remarkable achievements' and the necessity of her reign. As a result, a new post-decline ideology emerged, spanning all sides of Westminster. From sinking the *Belgrano* to hosting the Olympics, the media proclaims a British resurgence. Tony Blair cast the UK both as a 'pivotal power' between Europe and the US, and as 'cool Britannia', a trendsetter in fashion and retail. The colonies have gone; but Britain retains its purpose, and its intellectuals celebrate British Civilisation without apologies. Politicians and historians recount the Victorian era as a golden age, with lessons for American statesmen today. 'We should be proud of our colonial history in Africa,' Gordon Brown remarked on a trip to Tanzania, 'the days of Britain having to apologise for its colonial history are over.'[1]

In common parlance, 'British nationalism' refers to little Englanders, xenophobes and the BNP. But this confuses nationalism with defensive parochialism; for the most powerful states, nationalism affirms their right to rule. By this logic, Brown beats Nick Griffin or Nigel Farage as a British nationalist. True, Britain no longer commands other nations; instead, Westminster nationalism declares a continuous bond between the UK and US Empires. Their shared mission is to open closed societies to globalisation: 'commerce, civilisation and Christianity', in the words of Scottish explorer David Livingstone. British nationalists see uninterrupted purpose in the Anglophone world, a project to spread civilisation across the globe.

We call this the fantasy of 'Anglobalisation', following the Scottish historian Niall Ferguson.[2] This word captures both parts of British nationalism: the aristocracy of English-speaking whites, and free market evangelism. Although Ferguson's rhetoric recalls Tory chauvinism, all major parties in Westminster express similar ideas. This new British nationalism refuses to apologise for the past, and casts itself as a wise counsel to the American 'colossus'.

By explaining these ideas, we do not excuse them. Britain's Empire was far from a civilising influence. We refer anyone who doubts this to Mike Davis's research on 'late Victorian Holocausts', free market famines imposed on India and China in the late nineteenth century that killed up to 50 million.[3] We could mention the slave trade, Trevelyan's starving of Ireland, the Bengal famine, torture camps, and many other cruelties inflicted under the banner of 'civilisation'. Alas, we do not have the space to explore the details of Britain's crimes. But they are not ancient history or irrelevant to the debate. Gulags rendered 'Communism' unspeakable; the Holocaust did the same for fascism. Britain committed parallel acts in a parallel era, but nobody apologises. Instead, the Empire's achievements are heralded as exemplars of civilised rule.

In Chapter 2, we will examine British nationalism in greater depth. In this chapter, we want to confront the myth of post-Thatcher revival. Each proposal to 'fix' British decline, rather than adjust and transform Westminster's *raison d'être*, generates new imbalances. The product of these failed fixes is the constitutional crisis of 2014.

Imperial Crisis

As of 1909, the British Empire spanned a quarter of the world's surface, comprising 12.9 million square miles of territory and 444 million subjects. Including the oceans, Britain ruled 70 per cent of the planet.[4] Circa 1970, a small fraction remained. Although Britain intervened in ex-colonies such as Uganda, where it patronised Idi Amin, and in Northern Ireland, its sovereignty ran to a few islands. The Suez crisis was as damaging for British imperialism as Vietnam was for the Americans; for at least a generation, Westminster laboured under a 'Suez syndrome'. A significant bloc of Tory opinion, led by Enoch Powell, urged Westminster to adjust to the loss of Empire by retreating into insular English nationalism.

Thatcher's role was to mix Powell's English individualism with a muscular role for Britain in world affairs. When the Argentinian junta claimed sovereignty over the Falklands, her immediate response was to dispatch the naval fleet. Britain, Thatcher insisted, would not take impertinence from trumped-up generals. The affair helped Westminster overcome its Suez syndrome by showing that Britain could move unilaterally to defend its interests.[5] It also cemented a new transatlantic alliance with the Reagan administration, spanning the globe from Afghanistan to Chile in a war on socialism in any form.

The crusading US-UK alliance continued after the end of the Cold War. Blair emphasised the UK's role as 'deputy sheriff'[6] to the US in defending Western values, aiming to fuse Thatcher's brute force with so-called 'humanitarian purpose'. His advisers spoke of a 'post-modern imperialism' tasked with bringing freedom to the world.[7] Blair insisted: 'We are not a superpower, but we can act as a pivotal partner ... a force for good ... I believe we have found a modern foreign policy role for Britain.'[8]

The twin myths of humanitarian intervention and an ethical foreign policy helped to legitimise this benign imperialism. Charity-inclined celebrities such as Bono and Bob Geldof were happy to declare common purpose with US and UK leaders, who were 'good guys'. Bush and Blair, they insisted, wanted the G8 summit to rid Africa of hunger and disease. Even leaving Iraq aside, this strained credulity. Live Aid in 1985, the pinnacle of rock-star charity, raised £30 million to relieve African poverty. Two months later, the UK government finalised an arms deal with Saudi Arabian dictators worth £43 billion, more than 1,400 Live Aids.[9] Appeals to the moral character of world leaders can mask the systemic nature of violence.

But when Blair insisted that the UK directed American power to moral ends, he had many accomplices in the media. John Pilger, Seumas Milne and Tariq Ali may have queried this Westminster self-image, but there were few other dissenters. Of course, there were sprinklings of truth among the canards: the UK was more than a 'poodle' of the US. At the level of diplomacy and, to a degree, of armed force, Britain exercised potent force. Having once ruled the world, the UK is still one of five countries to have a permanent seat on the UN Security Council, along with the US, France, Russia and China. Even so, the term 'special relationship' is a Westminster vanity; the US's total military spending dwarfs all of its rivals put together (see Figure 1.1). Measured by arms superiority, the US surpasses any earlier Empire, even Britain at its peak.

The early years of the War on Terror appeared to cement American command. After 9/11, most agreed that terrorists had wronged America, and gave Washington leeway to exact vengeance, overriding international law. Only a few broke with conformity and identified the roots of 9/11 in American foreign policy. Afghan casualties, 'collateral damage' of the war, served as proof that justice requires sacrifices. The radical Left, and the odd Establishment deviant, opposed the war, but they were minorities; even the Scottish Nationalists praised the sincerity of Western intentions in Kabul.

The great gamble was to extend this ideological success to Iraq. Tony Blair knew the impact of the invasion would define the next generation of global politics. In the run-up to war, on 18 March 2003, he faced his critics in the Commons:

> The outcome of this issue will now determine more than the fate of the Iraqi regime and more than the future of the Iraqi people ... It will determine the way Britain and the world confront the central security threat of the 21st century; the development of the UN; the relationship between Europe and the US; the relations within the EU and the way the US engages with the rest of the world. It will determine the pattern of international politics for the next generation.[10]

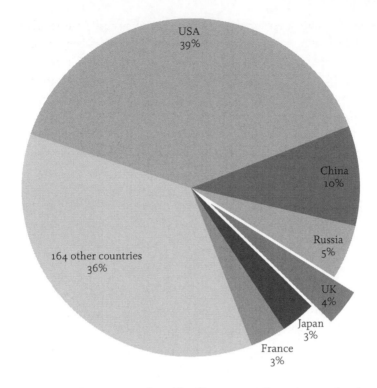

Figure 1.1   Percentage of world military expenditure in 2012 by six countries with highest expenditure

Source: Stockholm International Peace Research Institute (SIPRI) www.sipri.org

Today, the anti-Iraq War movement has changed the debate on American power. But in 2003, the establishment still accepted the framework of the US's good intentions. All Westminster parties agreed that Saddam's WMDs were the principle danger to world peace, and required swift action. Anyone who mentioned oil interests, queried WMDs, or cited Israel's nuclear bombs was labelled a conspiracy theorist or a lunatic.

This did not prevent many MPs voting against invasion, but the Lib Dems and other opponents still upheld the mission's sincerity, never questioning Bush's crusade against terrorism, chemical weapons and evil dictators. Their aim was a multilateral compromise and a second UN resolution. Those who moved outside this frame, such as Tony Benn and George Galloway, faced vicious character assassinations. 'Legitimate' opponents of the war preserved polite fictions of humanitarian purpose.

However, Blair's omen proved fatally correct: Iraq really did redefine global politics, even more than he imagined. After a decade of occupation, no one accepts US good intentions *a priori*, at least not without significant qualifications. Few doubt the anti-war version of events: that the neocons aimed to capture Iraq's oil ahead of Russia and China, and to strengthen Israel. Even Alan Greenspan, former head of the US Federal Reserve, admits as much: 'I am saddened,' he wrote, 'that it is politically inconvenient to acknowledge what everyone knows: the Iraq war is largely about oil.'[11]

Like Vietnam and Suez before it, Iraq looms over any US-UK mission. Opinions also shifted on Afghanistan, which morphed from a good war into a graveyard. The US's aerial power can destabilise 'rogue states' and 'evil dictators' with ease, but it could not command a restless population allied to a determined guerrilla resistance.

The UK presented itself as the conscience of US power, drawing on its colonial experience of building local alliances to police civilian populations. But 'divide and rule' in Iraq and Afghanistan did not prove to be a pacifying principle. On the contrary, it prompted vicious sectarian reprisals and open civil war. The persistent conceit of post-Thatcher Westminster – that a US-UK alliance could bind morals to muscle – is exposed as another bromide of imperial power.

As a result, post-Iraq Britain lacks clear purpose. The US has moved on under Obama, but still asserts remote influence in Syria and Pakistan. On Assad, the UK enraged their Washington handlers by voting against military action, the first time Westminster had openly disobeyed American wishes since Suez. This was a bungled miscalculation rather than a deliberate affront, but it highlighted new insecurities about the UK's vassal role. Britain needs the US far more than vice versa; the White House can find willing accomplices with ease.

After a drubbing in Iraq, and after the Syria vote, could Britain transcend its client status? Could the UK instead define a 'humanitarian' global role? This would require momentous political will and upheaval. Britain's military functions are entwined with its big businesses, with crossovers in personnel and a complex of vested interests gluing them together. Ten per cent of British manufacturing is arms related, with 9,000 companies working in the defence sector. The UK has the second most lucrative arms industry in the world after the US; last year, it exported £11.4 billion of hardware.[12] A powerful lobby commits Britain to preserving a war-like state.

British capitalism is not equipped for pacifism. 'Peace is bad for business at BAE,' laments *Management Today*. 'The defence giant today reported a nosedive in annual revenues following cuts in the UK and America.'[13] The cuts resulted from the US retreat from Iraq. BAE Systems is the third largest arms company in the world, and Britain's biggest manufacturer, thanks to a muscular pro-American foreign policy and UK taxpayer subsidies.[14]

In 2014, Scotland has the first opportunity in UK history to vote against Britain's military-industrial complex. Independence would scrap Trident nuclear missiles, that monument to the US-UK alliance. The prospect of a Yes vote has already brought new calls for Britain to relinquish its permanent seat on the UN Security Council.[15] In the event of a Scottish split, 'RUK's relationship with its key allies and traditional defence partners, including its privileged relationship with the US' would end, according to a report by the House of Commons Foreign Affairs Committee. This 'could serve to fuel the views of some states that the RUK was a power in irreversible decline.'[16]

This prospect terrifies Westminster elites and their supporters, who insist everyone benefits from a 'strong Britain'. We reject this premise: retaining Britain's global prestige benefits the upper echelons of society at the expense of everyone else. A taxpayer-subsidised military hardware industry creates few jobs and little opportunities to raise living standards. What it supplies is regular profits, and a macho nationalist self-image.

So while the Westminster establishment bask in a jingoistic status quo, most of Britain suffers. In monetary terms alone, the cost of the war was enormous. Recent research shows the American taxpayer will spend $6 *trillion* on the 'War on Terror', surpassing spending on even the Second World War.[17] British costs run at more than £20 billion[18] (modest by comparison, but significant in an era of 'necessary' austerity). We should compare these figures to the genuine challenges to human security in the new century. As Bush and Blair whipped up a climate of emergency over Iraq, they concealed the urgent emergency of climate. We waste a scandalous amount of resources, and human beings, on the American alliance. But within Westminster, no alternatives are emerging.

The Economy

After Thatcher's death, commentators spoke of her divided legacy. On the one hand, pundits argued, her authoritarian style alienated minorities and her neoliberal policies caused social problems and high unemployment. But most also 'grudgingly accept' that Thatcher's economic medicine worked. Britain *had* been in need of reform, they observe, due to uncompetitive industry and trade union power. Brutal as her methods were, Thatcher helped the UK overcome decline and become a competitive economy. The task of succeeding governments has been to include people in the prosperity she created, not to undo her work.

This consensus prevailed even before her death. New Labour paid homage to her economic record, and SNP leaders chimed in. As Alex Salmond told Conservative blogger Iain Dale:

> I suppose I have tried to bring the SNP into the mainstream of Scotland. We have a very competitive economic agenda. Many business people have warmed towards the SNP. We need a competitive edge, a competitive advantage – get on with it, get things done, speed up decision making, reduce bureaucracy. The SNP has a strong social conscience, which is very Scottish in itself. One of the reasons Scotland didn't take to Lady Thatcher was because of that. *We didn't mind the economic side so much. But we didn't like the social side at all.*[19]

The British establishment claim they are divided over Thatcher's legacy, but the opposite is true. Thatcher fostered undesirable 'social exclusion', but also an economic renaissance. Without her brutal methods, Britain might have declined further; instead, it re-branded as a hip, hi-tech exemplar of a service-led economy. Although there are outright opponents and enthusiasts, a conformist middle ground prevails, but does this capture the reality of Thatcher?

In truth, even by narrow capitalist standards, Thatcher failed to 'make Britain great again'. In 1979, Britain ranked sixth among world economies; it occupied the same position a decade later. The UK rose above the Soviet Union, but fell behind Italy.[20] Sound money, for Thatcher's chancellor Nigel Lawson, was the 'judge and jury of a government's record'.[21] But Thatcher's central economic claim – that she beat inflation – is contestable. When she left office, inflation stood at 9.7 per cent; a smidgen lower than when she started (10.3 per cent).

For these qualified gains, Thatcher sacrificed growth, which averaged a mere 1.75 per cent and never rose above a couple of points in her reign. This record was as bad, perhaps worse, than the 1970s, that dismal decade of 'decline'; but unlike Heath, Wilson, or Callaghan, Thatcher benefited from the huge bounty of North Sea oil, which in the early 1980s accounted for 8 per cent of government revenue. Overall public spending was 42 per cent of GDP when she left office, the same as when she began.[22] Ironically, Thatcher presided over a falling ratio of private sector employment, since her emphasis on strong money led to a slump in manufacturing jobs.

Using more substantive measures, Thatcher left a weakened economy. In earlier decades, analysts assessed Britain's economic health by its balance of payments. 'Britain in the red' meant imminent economic doom. Politicians made and lost careers due to this key measure of power and prestige. The Thatcher years ended with a non-oil current account deficit of £4.5 billion;[23] it should have been an emergency. By rights, bankers should have been jumping off skyscrapers, but Thatcher's regime jettisoned measures of economic success if they did not suit Tory interests. For Lawson, the pink book was not a constraint on Britain's economy, but was rather

> ... entirely the result of private individuals and businesses making choices about their own financial affairs ... provided the firm financial framework is in place, a period of private sector induced current account deficit should give no cause for concern, particularly given this country's exceptionally high levels of net overseas assets.[24]

This change of focus, resulting partly from ideology and partly from necessity, continued in the Major and Blair governments. By 2006, the balance of payments deficit reached a whopping £43 billion, but no one panicked. Thatcher's greatest victory was changing how economic success was measured. Even by her chosen criteria, though, her record was far from exemplary.

Thatcher's true accomplishments lie in deregulating the debt economy. These shifts were real, albeit romanticised in nostalgic accounts of yuppies and the Big Bang. Britain's perceived renaissance derives from the City of London's leadership in the market for financial wizardry. But was this producing new wealth? Once we strip away its mystifying glamour, the successes of this sector result from anti-social activities, from asset stripping, to privatisation, to tax evasion. Meanwhile, deregulated credit, allied to low wages, flooded the economy with debt. This funnelled investment into retail and speculation, while industrial capacity stagnated.

Thatcher's more intelligent supporters claim that she did the dirty work and laid foundations for success. But later governments fared little better.

Average income grew 2.4 per cent per year in the lean 1960s and 1970s; but only 1.7 per cent in the two decades since 1990.[25] And much 1990s growth was 'false', that is, caused by credit and housing booms. In 18 years of Tory rule, private borrowing increased by 50 per cent. But in only ten years of Labour, it jumped by close to 75 per cent. Under Blair, total private-sector debt nearly doubled, from 133.5 per cent to 227.4 per cent of GDP.[26] Once we subtract this bubble, analysts observe, the UK economy stood still.

The aftermath to this blowout has been a £1.2 trillion bank bailout, which could throttle Britain for a generation. Economists predict another decade of negligible growth, and Con-Dem austerity is intensifying decades of failure. British recovery, up to now, has been non-existent: averaging negative 0.2 percent since 2008, the UK boasts among the worst growth rates of any advanced Western economy. The US, by comparison, has grown by an average 2 per cent. Despite a weakened Euro, European rivals bettered the UK post-crisis: growth in Germany has averaged 0.7 while France also moved forward as the UK slipped back.[27]

For decades, British intellectuals lectured other countries about our service-led miracle. Even Alex Salmond embraced the mystical cult of British economics. But commentators are starting to recognise that, compared to the club of capitalist nations, the UK is unfit. Indeed, *Guardian* economics editor Larry Elliott argues that Britain has 'Third World' development problems. Its areas of strength – financial speculation, public relations and the arms industry – are also sources of the most severe instability, and none of them are useful to society. Britain, suggests Elliott, bases its economy on 'banking and bullshit' (to which we would add 'bombs'). He asks:

So what is Britain good at? ... The Germans may have the engineers, the Japanese may know how to organise a production line, but the Brits have the barristers, the journalists, the management consultants and the men and women who think that making up jingles and slogans in order to flog Pot Noodles and similar products is a serious job. It has the deal-makers in the City who make fat fees by convincing investors to launch bids for companies, and the corporate spin doctors who tell former pals in financial journalism that tycoon X will make a better fist at running Ripoff plc than tycoon Y ... The four iconic jobs in 21st-century Britain, according to a thinktank called the Work Foundation, are not scientists, engineers, teachers and nurses, but hairdressers, celebrities, management consultants and managers.[28]

Britain's economic model has reached its limits after 2008. To progress, it must break with its areas of highest success, such as finance and business services plus the arms industry. Over-reliance on these sectors has created a host of problems, from the bank bailouts to the culture of massive tax evasion, consumer indebtedness, and the foreign ownership of large parts of industry. Economies built on this model look dangerous and insecure in the present climate.

Of course, when people say Britain occupies a position of 'global leadership', they are correct. The most reactionary sectors in Europe envy the ease with which Westminster extorted wealth from the working class. Jingoists, frustrated aristocrats and high financiers in every European country would love to imitate Britain, which led the world in a neoliberal direction where citizens' livelihoods were treated as overheads. Why Scotland should vote to legitimise this settlement is another matter.

The Social Crisis

Thatcher cared very little about the social impact of economic reform. In the words of Tory chancellor Norman Lamont, high unemployment was a 'price worth paying' to tackle inflation. Restoring British power meant exposing as much of the country to the market as quickly as possible. The results, as even her admirers admit, were 'broken' communities and neglect. 'The Left are right to put part of the blame for the current riot of selfishness on the shoulders of Lady Thatcher,' says conservative pundit Peter Hitchens. 'They are right to perceive a moral emptiness in her government, which showed no interest in moral and cultural issues, in family breakdown, the decay of marriages, the collapse of discipline and learning in schools.'[29] Even Tories concede that Thatcher's reforms 'excluded' many British communities. New Labour aimed to remedy this by including them in the new prosperity of global markets. This is the essence of what Anthony Giddens, their court sociologist, called the 'Third Way'.

Under Blair, Labour scrapped Clause IV's pledge to nationalise industries and equalise incomes, but they always insisted they were finding new, and better, ways to achieve social justice. Government would act to remove artificial barriers to top careers, allowing women and people from working-class backgrounds to become investment bankers and CEOs. Even if income and wealth was unequal, lowly origins would be no obstacle to filthy riches. New Labour re-branded as a 'party of opportunity', and committed itself to meritocracy.

Sometimes, Labour conceded that status and social background barred access to elite jobs. But more often, a Westminster consensus said that class was no longer a real factor, any more than telegrams, rickets, or skiffle. 'The class war is over,' Blair announced.[30] Where inequality persisted, it resulted from barriers to the market's normal functioning, not market failure. Hence, the role of government was to aid private initiative, not to substitute for it. Pockets of dire poverty required targeted government action, using the welfare system to create incentives to join the job market.

New Labour accepted Thatcher's view that deprivation resulted from bad decisions, weak families and weak people. Rather than economic structure, they emphasised low self-esteem, alcohol and drug dependency, and absent fathers as causal factors. But they balanced this with expressions of concern for deserving victims. Children, in particular, should not be forced to suffer for the indolence and stupidity of their parents. The new Third Way morality said governments would not fund universal provision, as in post-war social democracy's blueprints and master plans. But it would target action where communities were rotten with neglect and criminality.

This entailed a close bond between social policy and penal policy. 'Tough on crime, tough on the causes of crime', according to Blair's famous formula, which prefigured his rise to Labour leader.[31] In power, concern about crime prevailed over concern about causes, as Labour insisted their most loyal voters, the poor and 'excluded', needed the tough love of heavy policing and surveillance. They found ever more creative means tests and punishments for unemployed and disabled people to 'create incentives to work'. Prison numbers ballooned. Tabloid labels – 'chavs' and 'scroungers' – defined policy priorities, in the name of reconnecting with voters.

This framework of social inclusion via 'tough love' has been Blair's lasting legacy. His success was to mould the Thatcherite narrative of winners and losers into a practical programme with the unthreatening language of fairness and justice. New Labour conceded that the miserable fate befalling its traditional supporters – trade unionists, industrial workers, council-house residents – was regrettable. But they had a simple message: shape up and modernise, or be punished, either by the market or by the law. This narrative was so convincing that it reshaped Westminster. Labour framed Thatcher's policies in inclusive vocabulary, forcing the Tories to spend a decade cleansing their nasty image. 'Hug a hoody' and 'red Toryism' resulted from this Blairite coup. All Westminster parties now share a broad, Third Way mindset that complements inclusion for strivers with sharp punishments for skivers.

Supporters of this consensus stress their paternalistic motives. Jail-time, workfare and benefit caps are meant to give the poor a 'hand up' and let them take part in new opportunities. But has a decade of these policies made any impact on social mobility? In truth, even Labour loyalists now concede failure on even these minimal counts. 'On Labour's watch, class has become more rigid, destiny for most babies is decided at birth, and the incomes of rich and poor families have drawn further apart,' admitted Polly Toynbee.[32] Sociologists differ on whether Britain's social mobility is in decline or remaining static. Studies suggest rates are falling, although measuring fluctuations is tricky. Nevertheless, the consensus states that Britain's statistics are grim for a developed country, and even Giddens, the founder of the Third Way ideology, admits that Britain's failure to tackle income divisions creates a sclerotic class system.

Skyrocketing inequality defines British politics since Thatcher, and the super-rich continued their ascent under Blair. Before the recession, the top 0.1 per cent of earners accounted for an amazing 5 per cent of total pre-tax income. Britain's richest 1,000 have £250 billion more than a decade ago, with overall trends towards *greater divisions* during the Blair years.[33] Since the 1970s, income inequality rose faster here than any other developed economy. This trend accelerated under New Labour's reign. 'The reason why there's been all this emphasis on social mobility is that all the political parties prefer to talk about social mobility and equality of opportunity rather than equality of conditions,' observes sociologist John Goldthrope.[34]

New Labour made these very minimal achievements, while allowing roaring inequalities, in fortuitous circumstances, with few recessions. As the boom-time ideology retreats, we get a clearer picture of the remains of UK society. Britain is the fourth most unequal country in Europe, ranked just ahead of crisis-ridden Greece, Italy and Spain.[35] Unemployment still stands at more than 2.5 million – well over 7 per cent.[36] Three-and-a-half million children, a full 27 per cent, endure relative poverty.[37] And a UN expert has called the UK's housing crisis a 'threat to human rights.'[38] Elementary physical needs are growing: hundreds of thousands are turning to food banks and homeless shelters.[39] Alongside Victorian-level inequality, new reports depict Victorian-level squalor. Statistically, Britain has among the most severe and traumatic social problems in Europe, and is often listed among the unhappiest nations.[40] Despite having held the reins of social policy for more than a decade, with a booming economy and a weak opposition, New Labour's achievements were slight at best.

Thanks to Thatcher, many saw Britain as a mean and uncaring society. Blair succeeded in changing this perception, by couching his pro-market philosophy in compassionate phrases. Now, with Labour out of power, the Con-Dem coalition has restored brazen elitism in Westminster; British politics has entered a 'Bullingdon Era'. Osborne, Cameron and Clegg stand for the true spirit of British capitalism; New Labour's jargon of inclusion justified the rewards of these same elites.

The Con-Dems made great strides in moving politics to the right with austerity. Ed Miliband, often regarded as a left-wing figure, says that Labour would be 'politically crackers' to spend what they did under Blair.[41] Although he makes the odd populist jibe at energy company fat cats and payday loan companies, he promises a leaner, meaner government, if elected. Austerity is discredited in academic terms. An American PhD student discredited the research government's cite to prove austerity's benefits, revealing numerous errors in an Excel spreadsheet.[42] But no Westminster party promises to shift course, despite five years of failure, despite the balance of intellectual argument. Hence, in a sense, Thatcher was right: in Westminster, there is no alternative.

New Labour said class divisions had vanished. In 'Cool Britannia', people moved fluidly between exciting new vocations, grabbing the opportunities of lifelong learning to become truly empowered and competitive global citizens. Status was no barrier: Eton toffs quaffed bitter in Wetherspoons and plumbers gobbled truffles from Waitrose. The task of reformers was a mopping -up exercise targeted to specific problem communities infested with low expectations, welfare dependency and criminality. There may be inequality, they observed, but there were enough opportunities for everyone.

By any measure, this narrative was a myth. As austerity scythes through the life chances of a generation, giving credence to these ideas is obscene. The evidence shows that where equality is greater, societies are more fluid, and people from humble backgrounds have more chance of success. No class-divided society is fair, but some are better than others. Unequal societies like Britain have no room at the top. By substantive measures, Third Way ideas are in tatters. But as an ideology, its influence is stronger than ever in Westminster.

The Democratic Deficit

An article of common sense says that a good society should create 'just rewards'.[43] Service to the public good should be rewarded; harming it should be punished. If this seems like elementary logic, it scarcely applies in Britain, where, in less than twenty years since 1993, the prison population in England and Wales nearly doubled from 44,500 to 85,000, despite crime *falling by half*.[44] There were no bankers, and only a few were politicians, among them, even as evidence mounted of their complicity, corruption and guilt. No wonder, then, that most Brits, and 58 per cent of Scots, believe 'there is one law for the rich, one for the poor.'[45]

It may seem farfetched to have Fred Goodwin et al. sewing mailbags in Barlinnie. But this happened to Icelandic bankers, whose risky and illicit dealings brought their economy to meltdown, and it was also the fate of 800 American bankers prosecuted after the 1980s Savings and Loan scandal.[46] What system of justice sends single mothers to jail for small council tax debts, while bankers get massive payoffs after bringing the country to ruin?

A similar logic applies for politicians. The MPs' expenses scandal exposed routinised criminality and corruption, but only a few were prosecuted. Meanwhile, young people have their lives ruined by jail time served for the pettiest of offences. Even authoritarian conservatives expressed indignation when London rioters were sent to jail for stealing bottles of water,[47] while most MPs received, at worst, de-selection with a huge pension for defrauding thousands of pounds. After all, aren't MPs supposed to set a better example for anomic youth? Tabloid newspapers are full of politicians aiming volumes of political vitriol at lax morals and declining standards in housing estates. As Frederick Forsyth, a Eurosceptic Tory pundit and monarchist, put it:

> When working class folk do something against the law it's a crime. That includes claiming benefits not entitled to, it's called theft. When politicians swindle the taxpayer by fiddling their expenses it is not theft at all, just an unfortunate oversight. If Old Etonians smash up the bar it is not hooliganism but youthful high spirits. Now the bankers have colluded to rig the Libor borrowing percentages and thus swindle the nation ... the next time I happen to be passing a bank robbery I shall get on the mobile, dial 999 and report that a behavioural lapse is taking place.[48]

Westminster's legitimacy problems are nothing new, nor are they unique to the UK. All societies have a democratic deficit. This problem has been heightened by the economic crisis, which exposed the weaknesses of politicians who could not, or would not, act to save public welfare from global bondholders. Who we vote for seems to matter less and less in this context, and mainstream politicians have been discredited. But while this rule applies across Europe, Westminster has faced the most precipitous collapse. Faith in UK politicians is even lower than the crisis-wracked economies of Southern Europe (see Figure 1.2). British people are less likely to trust their representatives than the Italians, who suffer near-annual corruption scandals, or the Greeks, whose politicians are a global byword for easy bribery.[49] Tellingly, support for Scottish independence is greatest when it is framed around the failings of Westminster.

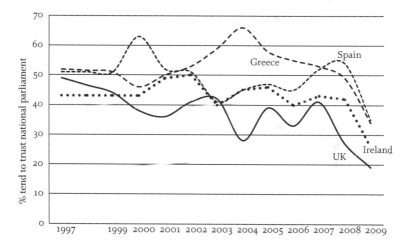

Figure 1.2   Trust in national parliament (% per year per country)

Sources: P. Norris, *Democratic Deficit: Critical Citizens Revisited*, Cambridge: Cambridge University Press, 2011, p. 74

Britain's pessimism has economic roots. Financiers are more likely to gain political office in the UK than in any other country except Switzerland. Indeed, even the US has fewer revolving door links between finance and government.[50] The Tories are monopoly-owned by bankers and financiers. Fifty per cent of their income comes from this sector, a total of over £6 million. This includes £1.38 million from hedge funds, £1.31 million from financiers, £1.16 million from fund/asset managers, and £0.61 million from bankers.[51] This is the party trusted to regulate the

City, that 'vital national interest', and to ensure no future meltdowns. The Square Mile floods Westminster with political donations; the rest of the economy, never mind working people, cannot compete.

Party funding, of course, is just one measure of Britain's larcenous politics. Corporate control of democracy goes far deeper. Examples also include scandals such as the News International affair, which included Alex Salmond as well as the Labour leadership, disclosing their seedy dealings and servility. Although outright bribery may be rare in British politics, it would be unnecessary. Westminster is already a wholly owned subsidiary of global corporations and billionaire tax exiles. When Murdoch's sway over political leaders, or the expenses scandal, is exposed, this does not cleanse Parliament, but merely serves to perpetuate public distrust and apathy.

Only a decade ago, there was so much optimism. Lord Irvine promised that New Labour would 'set out to be a Government which returns power to the people'.[52] Many believed them. Even leftists praised Tony Blair's government for reinvigorating the institutions of British democracy. In the *New Left Review*, Peter Mair argued that Labour was 'currently engaged in what amounts to a full-blooded constitutional revolution'.[53] Of course, even modest social change was off the agenda, but many were happy to compromise and see Labour as modernisers of the antiquated British state. The result would be a society in which birthright and privilege would be replaced by merit and representation – in politics, if not in business. Even if Labour was not taking on capitalist elites and financiers, at least it was ending foxhunting and it was shooing aristocratic relics out of the Commons and Lords.

The upshot was a patchwork of reforms masking much deeper continuities. Hereditary peers have almost vanished from the upper chamber, although a rump remains, and the Church of England bishops are still represented. However, plans for elections have been shelved; instead, the present hierarchy will continue, and Lords will be appointed by party-political patronage. Most would admit improvements over the earlier system: no one argues that ancestral land ownership is a good qualification for office. But this post-feudal modernisation has scarcely made 'democratic' institutions more vibrant.

Proposed replacements for the Lords have often verged on the barmy. Gordon Brown was obsessed with convincing celebrities, including Simon Cowell, Lorraine Kelly and Alan Sugar, to sit in the reformed Lords.[54] With ever-declining public faith in democracy, a sprinkling of celebrity pixie dust was the best Labour could offer. Tepid proposals for more serious electoral reform in Westminster have also been smashed, thanks to the disastrous coalition deal. When more democracy smells like more Nick Clegg, we must assume the proposal is dead for a generation.

The only true success of 'constitutional revolution' has been devolution. In the 1980s, Scottish and Welsh civic leaders spoke of a democratic deficit. A government they did not vote for dismantled their economies, and there seemed to be no recourse, since Thatcher centralised the British state beyond the dreams of post-war bureaucracies. The idea of devolved power, as devised by elements of the British liberal left, was to plug this gap and weatherproof British institutions. Those who designed the Scottish and Welsh Parliaments put safeguards in place to make sure these measures strengthened and reaffirmed British state power. Indeed, Labour thought they had engineered Holyrood to make a nationalist majority government impossible.

In many respects, devolution was too successful; against the wishes of its architects, it exposed all the faultlines of British politics. Arguably, the weakest link has been Labour itself. In Westminster, Labour's winning formula meant savaging traditional supporters while relying on fear of the Tories to whip constituencies into line. New Labour judged a policy's success by its aura in middle England (see Chapter 4). But devolution showed that, at least in Wales and Scotland, 'tribal' Labour voters would vote for anyone offering better policies, provided the threat of Tory rule was removed. In this sense, the two main Westminster parties depend on each other. Labour needs very little muscle to distinguish itself from the Tories in the eye of working-class voters. In a broader ecosystem of nationalists, greens and socialists, without the fear of Thatcherites and bigots, their countless intellectual and political flaws are exposed.

Many assert that the Tories would rule Westminster forever if Scotland gained independence. In technical terms, this claim is false, since Labour would have won majorities in 1945, 1950, 1997, 2001 and 2005 without Scottish votes. Indeed, Scottish MPs have only changed the result of elections on three occasions since the 1920s: 1964, 1974 and 2010. Only once in the last century has Scotland outright prevented a Tory government.[55]

But there are even more glaring flaws in the perpetual-Tory-rule thesis. In modern elections, the Conservatives have never managed to achieve half the votes across Britain, and they only commanded majorities due to Westminster's absurd arithmetic. The winner-takes-all election system forces all parties to fight for swing voters in marginal constituencies, rather than to raise the vote overall. So Labour policy is geared to a few million people, rather than raising participation in Britain as a whole. It assumes the compliance of core supporters, who will always fear the Tories, and focuses on closing down space on the right flank. Aiming to take back Labour, while rubbishing constitutional questions, is not an effective strategy for even minimal social change (see Chapter 4).

Moreover, overall neoliberal trends under Blair, as with Thatcher's policies, were not always popular. All sides of Westminster denied they could combat the rise of the super-rich. If this was the case, most of Britain disagreed: as the OECD observe, 65 per cent oppose current rates of inequality.[56] The problem is that no party represents this view. Until the fundamental form of British politics changes, this trend of weak representation will continue, and the democratic crisis will intensify. But a 'No' vote in 2014 solidifies this settlement for a generation.

Conclusion

Britain's national mythologies are starting to unravel. The guiding thread between these ideas is that the reforms of the 1980s, painful at the time, allowed Britain to enter the twenty-first century as a vibrant global power. While Thatcher may have wielded a hammer, the Blair years sought to entice all of Britain into this new settlement. On the one hand, the new prosperity created opportunities for anyone with the brains and the guts. Everyone could have a role in globalised Britain, whether as the investment banker, the barista pouring his latte, or the lapdancer relieving the strains of City life. But those who refused to shape up were unfit and needed a short sharp shock. There were no excuses left for missing out on obscene wealth. The rest of Britain is doing it – why not you?

Historical perspective, as we have said, is significant here. Britain threw off the image of decay, defeat and decline. Indeed, although this aura still lingers, it is a spectre; instead, intellectuals reassert Britain's colonial period as the morally just framework for all global civilisations, and post-war Britain is regarded as an unfortunate anomaly. New Labour and the Tories aimed to recover a sense of Victorian purpose, acting as a 'civilising' influence on the globe. The phantom unity of the English-speaking world, of the US-UK Empires, was the glue holding this together. The irony is that, despite the faults of the post-war era, it created the greatest social ease and opportunity in British history. Even the worst years of decline had higher growth and lower unemployment than the era of post-Thatcher recovery. For this reason, many on the Left yearn for the 'spirit of 45'.

But returning to Attlee-era priorities is inconceivable under present arrangements. Labour has been the most enthusiastic prosecutor of the new British nationalism and its punitive optimism. The election of Ed Miliband, perhaps far more than the Blair years, shows that 'taking back Labour' is a hopeless project. Miliband, after all, was the ideal Labour Left candidate: his father a Jewish Marxist professor, he won the leadership battle with union votes. While he is more sceptical than his predecessors about a globalising Britain, his scepticism is couched in a revived parochialism. Miliband criticises New Labour for not accepting that one part of globalisation – immigration – harmed the white working class. He promises to return to that seedy underbelly of New Labour's nationalism: 'British jobs for British workers'. For now, Labour stresses the Anglo in Anglobalisation, as the right of white Protestants to their share assumes priority over gunboat diplomacy.

This turn from Anglobalism to a more exclusive Britishness is an inevitable result of the austerity era, with the UK adapting to lean times. 'No growth, high unemployment, deep cuts, and little hope', was how Adam Shaw put it on BBC's *Panorama*.[57] The heady years before Iraq and the bailouts, the era of 'Cool Britannia', multiculturalism and easy credit, are distant memories. Instead, we have the perverse reassertion of privilege in politics: the social privilege of Eton elites, and the ethnic privileges of white Britishness. Westminster is making room for UKIP, a coalition of stockbrokers and chauvinists, in a signal of this new politics.

Optimistic British nationalism, in all its elements, relied on myths. The geopolitical myth pitched Britain as a 'pivotal partner' between Europe and America, bringing human rights and civilisation to the world. The economic myth said banking, bombs and bullshit could replace factories. The social myth viewed markets as a lever to involve 'excluded' groups in Britain's new prosperity. And the democratic myth said the UK's constitutional revolution would remove privilege from politics. Today, each faces its own crisis. These fractures now centre on Scottish independence and the referendum of 2014.

Even if Scotland votes No in 2014, Britain's constitutional crisis will persist. The problems are interlocking. Britain's economic form and its global strategy are linked, as financial and military elites both benefit from the same neoliberal consensus. Social inclusion failed because there was no way of bringing people into this order. Britain spends a huge amount subsidising military industries, the armed forces and the banks, while neglecting to invest in infrastructure and welfare. And Westminster's democratic malaise reflects all three of these problems. The fiascos of UK politics stem from incurable maladies in its political economy, and the current crisis of British nationalism is far from an accumulation of chance events. A No vote resolves nothing; it will merely guarantee the certainty of uncertainty.

2

British Nationalism: The Missing Link

As we explained, the reassertion of Britishness has created new insecurities. Although images of patriotic fervour, from the Olympics to the Royal baby, flood the public sphere, Project Britain faces severe crises, even by its preferred measures. Having explored the elements of crisis in depth, we will now develop the idea of Britain itself. Many assume Britain's meaning is already clear, but in truth, its identity is opaque and clouded in ideology.

'Great Britain,' argues leading Tory MP David Willetts, 'provides the political institutions which link these two nations [Scotland and England] in above all an outward-looking endeavour of trade and conquest – it is the British Army, the British Empire and the British pound'.[1] Willetts' formula, which would accord with the Anglobalisation concept, has ingredients of truth. But there are many other meanings attached to Britain, from warm beer and cold weather to the monarchy, the BBC and the NHS.

Some contrast the welfarist idea of the British state with the conquest idea, but we doubt if this clarifies matters. As Tom Nairn notes, Labour has always been careful to frame the post-1945 settlement in terms of its *continuity* with the Empire form.[2] The welfare state was the *evolution* of Britain to include the working class in its prosperity, a 'just reward' for sacrifices in the World Wars. Thus, even in high socialist mode, the link between conquest and trade was in Britain's marrow.

Many people take offence at calling Labour's politics 'British nationalist', since the term has been confused by proximity to the National Front, the BNP and UKIP. We are not lumping mainstream Westminster together with these fringe groups. Indeed, we use the term with reluctance and after considerable agonising. But nationalism proved an unavoidable concept; unionist abuse of the term borders on perversion, and left us no choice. Examples of lame, uncritical diatribes against nationalism's evils abound. 'The politics of nationalism,' says Scottish Labour leader Johann

Lamont, is a 'virus that has affected so many nations and done so much harm'.[3] Avoiding the phrase 'British nationalism', for fear of the fascist connotations, allows these claims to pass without examination.

So while the media pores over the pathologies of Scottish nationalism, Britain's ruling ideologies receive cursory scrutiny. The absence of critique on this front weakens the standard of the 2014 debate on all sides. We feel this gives a jaundiced account of national identity and, more to the point, racism in Scottish society.

Thus, the Britishness of Scotland has warranted almost no attention, as against so-called 'separatist' impulses. 'It is not simply that Scottishness is part of Britishness,' observes sociologist Neil Davidson, 'it is also that Britishness is part of Scottishness and the latter would not exist, at least in the same form, without the former.'[4] Two nationalisms compete for loyalties in the referendum: Scottish and British. The second is the debate's missing link.

Farage and Salmond: Two Cheeks?

Nigel Farage, the leader of UKIP, is the darling of Britain's media. Since 2009, he has appeared on the BBC's flagship *Question Time* more than any other politician.[5] All this free publicity has helped to boost the party's support. In the last English local elections his party polled 25 per cent, putting it well above the Liberal Democrats. Given their controversial views, and their rise to prominence in England, one might expect detailed critical examination in the press. But the substance of his anti-immigrant agenda finds little resistance. Indeed, Farage's diatribes about a 'Romanian crime wave' and 'foreign criminal gangs' earn the plaudits of tabloid newspapers.[6] Even though his rhetoric targets the most vulnerable groups in British society, columnists praise his 'bravery'.

In June 2013, Farage tried to build on his electoral success by standing UKIP in an Aberdeen by-election. Despite receiving a flyspeck vote (0.28 per cent) in the Scottish council elections of 2012, he hoped for a breakthrough. But things did not go to plan. Protesters mobbed his first press conference on Edinburgh's Royal Mile, chanting slogans against UKIP's homophobic and anti-immigrant policies. Fleeing, Farage hopped in a taxi, but the driver refused to budge. The local constabulary locked the UKIP leader in a pub for his own safety, before bundling him into a nearby police wagon.

The media's reaction to the ensuing furore hinted at the 2014 debate's underlying concepts. Farage received meagre probing about his anti-immigrant politics, even though this was the substance of the protest and his party's key platform. Instead, his reading of the event, that it was 'the ugly face of Scottish nationalism', dominated the debate.[7] Although half the protesters, branded 'fascist yobbo scum' by Farage, were English, the press accepted UKIP's account and agonised over Anglophobia in the independence movement.

Even Farage's critics were quick to pounce on the Scottish Left's unresolved English issues. Hence, old Unionist socialists leapt to the defence of Britain's leading anti-immigrant agitator. His most prominent supporter was George Galloway, who railed against Anglophobia in the independence movement. He also admonished its 'anti-Irish' streak, and predicted that a Yes vote in 2014 would lead to pogroms against the Irish population.[8]

This restates the old Unionist bromide that Scottish nationalism is pathological. After the election of the first nationalist government at Holyrood, for example, senior Labour politicians, including Ian Davidson, Anne Moffat and Jim McGovern, attempted to link the SNP with 'neo-fascism', anti-English 'hatred' and Nazism.[9] Labour peer George Foulkes compared Alex Salmond to fascist dictator Benito Mussolini,[10] while MP Tom Harris resigned his position as Scottish Labour's social media guru after he released a video portraying the first minister as Adolf Hitler.[11]

Michael Moore, the former Lib Dem Scottish secretary, used his conference platform to compare Salmond to Farage. 'There is of course a clear parallel between those who want Scotland to leave the UK, and those who want the UK to leave the EU,' he said. 'For both the nationalists and the Eurosceptics, there is a hard need to assert a specific sense of national identity.'[12] This is a typical device of British liberalism. The *Guardian* front page following Farage's flight from Edinburgh depicts a face-off between Salmond and the UKIP leader under the headline 'Battle of Nationalists'.[13] Here, the elements of contemporary British ideology are clear: the three mainstream parties of 'Better Together' – the Tories, Lib Dems and Labour – do not depend on any specific sense of national identity, and they are not nationalist. Nationalism is a product of the UK fringes. Westminster politics, by an implicit contrast, is either neutral with respect to nationhood, or somehow 'internationalist'.

Examining Labour's claims shows just what neutrality means in this sense. In January 2012, Labour MP Willie Bain launched an attack on Alex Salmond's progressive credentials. 'Nationalism is, at it [sic] core, a deeply negative and regressive politics.' he explains. 'I care just as much about a child growing up in poverty in my constituency in Glasgow as I do a child in poverty in Liverpool, Cardiff, London, Aberdeen, Dundee or Edinburgh.'[14] This gives a succinct demonstration of British ideology. Following this logic, if Willie Bain opposes nationalism, he favours internationalism instead; in which case, this peculiar internationalism seems to include Cardiff and Liverpool but not Dublin, Athens, or Baghdad. The blackmail of this British globalism, which runs from John O'Groats to Land's End but seems to cover Atlantic alliances, is what remains of a 'Left' critique of Scottish independence. It repeats the Labourist equation where British patriotism equals value-free concern for humanity as a whole. As Tom Nairn argued, 'One can never be internationalist enough for a true British nationalist.'[15]

Patriots and Nationalists

George Orwell's distinction between good patriotism and bad nationalism has proved very influential. Many British commentators and politicians will thus contrast their harmless enthusiasm for Britain's land and people and 'unique' citizenship to the bloodthirsty nationalism of others (foreigners, Scots, UKIP). For sociologist Michael Billig, the British are not alone here; the same form applies to every official national ideology. He observes that 'Nationalism is not confined to social movements, which aim to create new nation-states, but it is also the ideology of established nations.'[16] But what he calls 'banal nationalism' is disguised in official discourse:

'Our' loyalties to 'our' nation-state can be defended, even praised. A rhetorical distinction is necessary for this defence. 'Our' nationalism is not presented as nationalism, which is dangerously irrational, surplus and alien. A new identity, a different label, is found for it. 'Our' nationalism appears as 'patriotism' – a beneficial, necessary ... force.[17]

The major irony of this can be seen if we return to Orwell, the granddaddy of patriotism. 'By "patriotism" I mean devotion to a particular place and a particular way of life, which one believes to be the best in the world but has no wish to force on other people,' he claims. 'Patriotism is of its nature defensive, both militarily and culturally.'[18] By contrast, for Orwell, nationalism is about dominance and hierarchy. The nationalist wants power, not for himself, but for the national unit. In Chapter 1, we outlined how the contemporary Westminster discourse is framed by the problem of national power. Of course, this has a modifying element: Atlanticism. When Labour and others claim they are internationalist, they mean they are committed to the special relationship and accepting of their role as an American underling. The British loyalties of Westminster parties, in any case, are clearly nationalist in the sense Orwell intended, while many so-called Scottish nationalists are much closer to Orwell's patriotism.

A dichotomy between (good) Scottish patriotism and (bad) British nationalism is unhelpful, though. As we will explain, Scottish patriotism – 'harmless' pride in belonging to the land and its people – sometimes regurgitates, by unconscious processes, the violence of British nationalism. Scottish patriotism becomes (bad) nationalism, as Orwell meant it, when it involves a heritage of conquest and aspirations to power. Precisely because Scotland is part of Britain, our patriotism is complicated, and freeing it from its Empire heritage requires negotiation.

Instead, we must build an internationalist approach, while being wary of the term's many abuses. We may start by looking at the state's actions, not who they claim to represent (Willie Bain's 'my constituents in Glasgow'). True internationalists understand that the dangers posed by loyalties to existing states are much greater than the dangers of establishing new ones. British nationalism is all the more dangerous for being invisible. Often covert, always banal, allegiances to powerful states have created the greatest crimes of nationalism in history: the most horrific example being the First World War. The hazards of new states are piffling by comparison.

We admit that loyalty to the British state is not just a tale of Blimpish nostalgia for Empire and Protestant privilege. Many people believe in its progressive mission for worthy reasons. In a recent article, *Guardian* columnist Jonathan Freedland hailed the 'heartfelt patriotism' of the London Olympics, arguing that the event's success halted historic British decline, and claiming that now 'we should love the country we have become.'[19] His aim was to defend multiculturalism and tolerance, not to sink the *Belgrano*. Again, when Tony Benn and others on the Labour Left railed against EEC entry in the name of British sovereignty, it was not because they glorified Britain's brutality in Ireland. It was because they felt, with touching naivety in retrospect, that the British state was distinctively socialist. In a similar fashion, left-wing unionists hark back to the 'spirit of '45', when the British state had something to offer working people.

Many have genuine and sincere hopes that Westminster can restore the promise of a better future. No matter how far the NHS or the Royal Mail is privatised, elements of these loyalties persist. If only the right leader would emerge! Despite the course of recent Holyrood elections, Scots are still lulled by the prospect of Labour government. Polls conducted in October 2012 showed that 56 per cent of Scotland would vote for independence if they believed the next UK regime would be Conservative.[20] Despite more than a decade of Blair, Scots still expect Labour to deliver clear improvements over Tory rule.

These caveats aside, compromising with any British nationalism is a poor choice. In recent decades, the progressive elements of welfare nationalism have been cut to the bone. Loyalties are preserved by jollying the population into a mean-spirited nationalism of the *Belgrano*-sinking variety. British values are mobilised against 'enemies within' as well as external enemies. Internal foes have included such unpatriotic menaces as Arthur Scargill, of course, and Labour used the same rhetoric against striking firefighters in the context of the Iraq War. Indeed, a Scottish Labour minister resigned after calling these working-class heroes 'fascist bastards'.[21]

It was Labour who coined the phrase 'British jobs for British workers', one of many solicitations to tabloid chauvinism. Labour Home Secretaries such as Jack Straw encouraged apocalyptic fantasies about refugees and immigration. But nothing compared to the opprobrium heaped on the 'unpatriotic' Muslim community in Britain after 9/11. Islamophobic vitriol was sweeping and unrelenting. Scare stories seeped from Westminster and thirsty tabloids lapped them up. Every day, new 'terror threats' emerged; every day, another Labour minister was eager to oblige with a quote.

Many Labour sympathisers blame this on Blair's betrayal of Old Labour values, but this belief stems from nostalgia, not facts. Old Labour in government more than matched New Labour's jingoism. Jim Callaghan imposed virginity tests for Asian women coming into the country.[22] Eugenics was a favourite topic of Fabian 'socialists', who wished to improve the nation's breeding stock.[23] Elements of the Labour Left, while less likely to support explicit racism, were, to say the least, naive about the Empire and the Commonwealth. Thomas Johnston, the legendary Scottish secretary of state, was a leading figure on the Left and a fanatical Empire enthusiast. He insisted that it 'might be the greatest lever for human emancipation the world has even known'.[24]

Scottish Labour MPs, including John Wheatley and James Maxton, also felt that 'the Empire was too big to be left to the Carlton Club.'[25] While many still idealise the Attlee era for establishing the welfare state, its record on colonial matters was dire. Attlee's government moved to block any United Nations oversight into its colonies, leading H.N. Brailsford, a Labour intellectual, to admonish them for upholding Britain's prerogative to 'wallop its own niggers' (quoting from Joseph Chamberlain).[26]

We do not wish to pick on Labour here. We should not forget that Keith Joseph, the mentor to Margaret Thatcher, withdrew from the Tory leadership race after hailing eugenics.[27] Thatcher surrounded her government with Blimpish fantasists and para-fascists.

Wherever we look, Westminster's British nationalism is inescapable. Its trajectory and its nature should form part of the debate on 2014; but even cursory mentions are rare. While Yes Scotland and the SNP are forced to defend themselves against charges of anti-English racism, Better Together leaders are never quizzed on their 'patriotism'. The ironic effect has been to make critiques of Scottish national identity sterile and limp. The Britishness of Scottish politics is unavoidable. Framing these problems as 'good' patriotism versus 'bad' nationalism just causes confusion. It evades the real problem: Scottish identity is dangerous because it derives from a Unionist sense of Protestant privilege. Scottish nationalism and unionism share ingredients in common.

Racism and Reaction in Scotland

In 2001, Kurdish refugee Fursat Dag was fatally stabbed as he returned home from a night out in Glasgow. The UK Border Agency had dispersed Dag, like many others fleeing persecution, to Sighthill, amid concerns at far-right activity in the South-east of England.[28] The murderer was white, and motivated by bigotry, although this evaporated in the trial.

Dag's death was one of many examples of racist violence in Scotland. Although the BNP and UKIP might not have an audience, there are regressive ideas across Scottish society. Our communities are not always hospitable or 'internationalist' as many claim. When we consider Scottish independence, we should take this into account. But the leaders of the independence debate want to avoid these tetchy topics. For Yes Scotland, racial intolerance is something that happens elsewhere. For the forces behind Better Together, one racism, and only one racism, matters: anti-English racism.

The Scottish media is likewise obsessed with this one brand of bigotry. Farage was not alone in raising alarm at Anglophobia; the papers love a sermon on the topic. Government figures in December 2012 showed a big increase (24 per cent) in white-on-white attacks. 'Anti-English rhetoric is at risk of "creeping" into Scottish society,' warned the *Daily Telegraph*.[29] Lib Dem, Labour and Tory voices implied that the referendum stoked these hatreds. Other newspapers leapt on this angle. 'Don't hate the English,' urged the *Daily Record*. 'Bigots exposed: MSPs want action against Scotland's mindless minority.'[30]

The controversy forced the Scottish government to release more detailed statistics, showing attacks on English people had *fallen* by 17 per cent.[31] Although they are the largest minority in Scotland, of a total of 1,295 racist incidents against whites, only 70 targeted the English. Most white-on-white attacks hit the Irish, while Polish people and Gypsy travellers also suffered abuse. Pakistanis, of course, comprised the largest number of victims.

None of this suggests that Anglophobia is acceptable; like any bigotry, it should command our vigilance. But the media misconstrues the volume of racism in Scotland, and this creates a subconscious frame for the 2014 debate. 'Anti-English racism has become the default position of a lot of right-wing folk trying and failing to import this or that piece of ideology,' notes Ian Bell.[32] Islamophobic and anti-Irish violence is routine 'slow news', while anti-English racism is a contentious, politicised, and – dare we say it – sexy topic.

Perceptions about 2014 are shaped by these unjustified priorities. If we treat Anglophobia as the main problem, we look for bigotry's roots in Scottish separatism. But if we examine where most racism occurs – with its Irish, Muslim and Eastern European victims – we are forced to interrogate Scotland's links to Westminster ideology. The media does not reflect reality; but it shapes perceptions and sets agendas. Hence, nobody questions Better Together on whether their parties' common history of immigration-baiting has led to an upsurge in Scottish racism.

Scotland's middle classes, expressing endless concern about Anglophobia, are bored by the Irish question. Discrimination against Irish immigrants is history, they argue; what remains is the (religious) problem of 'sectarianism'. This attitude prevails despite Scotland's documented legacy of 'religious' apartheid. Scottish institutions are starting to confront this on a piecemeal basis. Just a decade ago, the Church of Scotland admitted to anti-Irish 'racism akin to the "rivers of blood" speech of Enoch Powell in the 1960s'.[33] In the 1920s, the Kirk sent a letter to the Scottish secretary claiming: 'A law-abiding, thrifty and industrious race [the Scots] is being supplanted by immigrants [the Irish], whose presence tends to lower the social conditions and undermine that spirit of independence which has so long been a characteristic of the Scottish people.'[34]

But this past is only addressed in the murkiest terms. The official discourse, peddled by both Unionists and nationalists, is that Scotland has a sectarian problem. Jack McConnell called it 'Scotland's secret shame'; likewise, the SNP take every opportunity to push an 'anti-sectarian' agenda. This serves to elide the systematic discrimination against immigrants which defined Scottish politics for generations. Moreover, it glosses the ideology underlying this: Protestant privilege and Empire superiority, the elements which attached Scots to the British state. As Finn observes, the notion of sectarianism:

> ... avoids any identification of causality, neglects any analysis of social and political power within Scotland and implies equal culpability for prejudice between majority and minority communities and helps retain the myth of Scotland as a democratic and egalitarian society, free from the stain of racism. Much that is claimed to be sectarianism is better described as anti-Irish racism.[35]

Of course, while many couch this in euphemisms, others are outright denialists. Pundits often urge Scots of Irish descent to cease their whining. Stewart Cosgrove, one of Scotland's leading media commentators, snapped: 'Lame attempts by Celtic fans to elevate the potato-throwing incidents into the realm of racial prejudice is a pathetic and intellectually bankrupt idea. In modern Scotland, *anti-Irish racism has virtually disappeared*.'[36]

The Irish do not face unique discrimination in Scotland. True, Scots of Irish descent have far more chance of ending up in jail, or suffering health problems.[37] However, other groups encounter far greater discrimination today. Irish Catholics achieved official employment parity in 1991, albeit it took 90 years longer for them in Scotland than it did in America. How many Muslims, Indians, Africans, or East Europeans are in Scotland's top jobs? None of these groups are well represented in the independence campaign, on either side. Nor are they likely to find themselves on the board of Scottish companies or quangos. By contrast, English people move with ease into Scotland's upper echelons.

In 2012, pundits lambasted Scotland's greatest novelist, Alasdair Gray, after he released a rant against English 'colonists' in the elite Scottish arts sector.[38] Doubtless, the terms of his attack were not well chosen. But it points to the felicity with which English people join the top, Protestant-dominated parts of Scottish society. The contrast with the experience of Scots Asians and other oppressed groups should be clear.

England does not colonise Scotland, and nobody should claim victim status as a badge of honour. But we would add a small caveat. The discourse of anti-English racism traces the bigotry of Scottish people to a sense of inferiority against the dominant Anglophone culture. By contrast, if we focus on the anti-Irish, anti-Pakistani, and so on, element, Scottish bigotry instead derives from a privileged aristocracy of Protestant Empire. This sense of withdrawn privilege causes racism at the bottom of society. We do not wish, for a second, to downplay any racism, but the focus on the anti-English element has clear class connotations. It contains, at a subconscious level, an anti-working-class discourse, unless qualified by recognition of other Scottish racisms.

Conclusion

For nationalists, sovereignty is its own reward. Although we do not deny any nation the right to decide its fate, our motives are not limited to this: we aim to change Scottish society. In the next chapter, we will examine the socio-economic structure of capitalist property in Scotland. The idea that Scotland has a social-democratic consensus is misleading and limits political initiative. In similar terms, the imaginary Scotland that always welcomes immigrants, with its 'civic' identity politics, is not everyone's experience. It would be a shame if tackling bigotry and other forms of discrimination did not form a major part of the debate in 2014. The adversarial mode of the debate squanders a crucial chance to confront the murkier details of Scottish identity. Both Yes and No campaigns are dominated by white men, reflecting a failure to confront oppression and privilege.

So loving Scotland need not conflict with unreconstructed British chauvinism. Scottish patriotism, if by this we mean pride in bagpipes, hillsides and kilts, can symbolise conquest, and those wishing to reclaim it must be wary. Indeed, historians have claimed that Scottishness was no more than a creation of Empire: an exaggeration, doubtless, but with a grain of truth.[39]

Scots today are still prone to the ugliest elements of neo-Britishness. The *Sun* is Scotland's most popular newspaper. Far more Scots read diatribes against immigrants, Muslims and other officially sanctioned enemies than read the *Herald*. Prejudiced views and racist political behaviour can diverge. English people held vile views in earlier decades ('No Irish, No Blacks, No Dogs'), but parties such as the National Front gained no foothold. As society-wide attitudes mellowed, extreme parties gained an audience. Things might move back the other way; attitudes to racism in England are hardening, as shown by endless programmes agonising about the white working class. By contrast, Scots do not vote for reactionary protest parties; but bigoted attitudes persist, without official recognition.

By saying that Britishness is central to Scottish bigotry, we do not exonerate Scotland. Indeed, we want to insist that Scottish nationalism is not separate from its British counterpart, but linked to it. After all, for decades, the SNP leadership had a sorry record on anti-Irish bigotry, which it began to confront in the mid-1990s. Many still associate it with Protestant privilege, and Salmond's attempt to criminalise Irish Republican politics, under a blanket anti-sectarian discourse, has made this worse. These issues reflect Scotland's role as a chief partner in the British Empire. The great industrial dynasties and the Scottish Tory-Unionist political structures may have gone, but British identity is stamped all over Scottish society. Voting Yes is a tentative step, a flight from Scotland's past of bigotry, violence and hatred.

3

Caledonia PLC:
Capitalist Power in Scotland

In 1707, Scotland surrendered sovereignty to embrace the economic benefits of Union with a larger neighbour. For Scotland's ruling barons, nationhood had a cash price, and three centuries on, the case for independence rests on similar calculations. Scots are not confronting oppressors, their rulers having joined with England's to conquer other nations. Nor are Scots reclaiming cultural rights, as in Wales. Perceptions about economic security will decide the 2014 referendum, with polls showing a huge majority of Scots will vote Yes if it guarantees better living standards.[1]

Hence, the Westminster establishment knocks Scotland's viability, and the media floods our public sphere with dire warnings of the risks of independence. What would we do about another bank collapse? What currency would we use? Can Scotland prosper without the City of London? This tactic is nothing new; the same questions dominated earlier debates about home rule. Ten days before the 1979 devolution referendum, a *Daily Express* editorial asked, 'How much of Scotland's economy will be left intact if a Scottish Assembly gets the go-ahead on March 1? Will our coal mines go gaily on? Will Ravenscraig or Linwood thrive? Will Bathgate flourish and Dounreay prosper?'[2]

The *Express* case was convincing: enough Scots voted No to prevent Home Rule for a generation. A decade later, having opted for Westminster's security, just one deep mine remained in Scotland. Linwood, a major car factory, closed in 1981, while its sister-project, the British Motor Corporation tractor and lorry plant at Bathgate, survived until 1986. The steel mill at Gartcosh closed the same year. A long-running cross-party campaign did not save the flagship Ravenscraig mill, which fell in 1991. Dounreay shut in 1994. Other notable closures included Singer in Clydebank, Massey Ferguson in Kilmarnock, the Invergordon smelter, and

Caterpillar in Uddingston. This industrial cataclysm came when North Sea oil should have guaranteed new prosperity. Instead, under Thatcher, its proceeds bankrolled tax cuts for the wealthy and the war on inflation.

In 1979, Scotland paid the price for voting No. The ability of ruling elements of Britain to cast doubt on the economy was a major reason behind this. Since then, nationalist responses to economic change in Scotland have taken two directions. One is the 'Letter from America' model, which presents the ravages of Thatcherism as the latest victimhood imposed on Scotland, a new Highlands Clearances. Scotland's dynamic with Britain becomes a continuous story of theft, lost rights and forced emigration. We should be wary of romantic temptations here: there never was a Golden Age of Scotland, and nostalgia for Scottish industry should be tempered by its imperial role, along with pollution, ill-health, overcrowding, bigotry, violence, low wages and the accompanying macho drinking culture.

Getting jollied into 'talking up' the Scottish economy is another trap. Many nationalists express faith that Westminster's gloom will be overcome by setting Scotland's enterprising spirit free. They point to new industries as evidence of renaissance, and say very little of Scotland's entrenched power elites and enduring inequalities. A series of model economies, from the 'Celtic Tiger' to the 'Arc of Prosperity', suggest the potential benefits of being a small nation in a competitive world. This model poses a real danger: an independent Scotland, under global neoliberalism, could face a 'race to the bottom' with low-wage peripheries.

Scotland has pockets of great wealth, and a prosperous capitalist economy. If independence happened tomorrow, Scotland would be the sixth richest OECD country, based on gross domestic profit per head, ahead of the UK (fifteenth).[3] Of course, qualifications are necessary: much of this wealth is owned overseas, and the profits made in Scotland are not benefiting most people's livelihoods. Private owners are squandering our vital resources, posing dilemmas about economic growth. Scotland's riches sit alongside pools of dire poverty: not just people living in relative poverty, but suffering from real physical deprivation in terms of housing and food. Growing Scotland's economy is one question, but the true problem is dividing the wealth – a political, not a technical issue.

Half of Scotland's land is owned by 432 people.[4] This natural wealth is vital to a green energy future, but people are still deserting the Scottish countryside because they have no economic future there. This shows the clear conflict of interest between Scotland's needs and the 'rights' of inherited property.

While critics point to hunting estates and ancestral landholdings, big business receives less attention. After losing so many industries, many assume that Scotland's capitalist class is weak or non-existent. In parliamentary terms, Scotland has no electable party dominated by business or landowner personnel. The Conservative/Unionists used to play this role, but their decline is irreversible. Their allies, the ruling firms and families of Scottish commerce a century ago, have also vanished. Holyrood's major parties proclaim left-of-centre beliefs, leading commentators to assume middle class, social democratic rule. Sociologist David McCrone offered a version of this thesis: 'Key groups in the Scottish class structure have dissented from the values of the Anglo-British state and of market liberalism to the extent that new political arrangements within that state grow increasingly likely.'[5]

In reality, devolution proved the opposite, as Scotland's socio-economic profile fused with the US-UK model. An ecosystem of pro-market think tanks created a conformist neoliberal consensus in the Holyrood village. And RBS/HBOS's takeovers and investments put the whole UK economy in jeopardy. Scotland's big business interests are instinctive enemies of a progressive economic alternative, having little to gain from social investment, and much greater links to transnational business than local communities. Without understanding these interests, radical blueprints for change will get nowhere.

Financialisation

Thatcher's policies put millions out of work and gutted much of the Scottish economy. She spoke of letting the market decide which industries were fit for survival, but in practice she often broke this rule. It was Thatcher, for instance, who considered the Scottish banking sector too big to fail. While mines, factories and steel mills closed, RBS's Edinburgh headquarters survived, thanks to a political decision rather than the free market.

By cold cash logic, Hong Kong-based HSBC should have swallowed RBS in a 1981 hostile takeover. Scotland would have lost one of its two major banking centres. But a patriotic coalition of the STUC, the Scottish Office and various politicians forced Thatcher to refer the bid to the Monopolies and Mergers Commission. RBS survived the 1980s because big government ruled that its Scottish identity served the national interest.

Scotland's later experiment in turbo-charged capitalism thus began with a rare Thatcherite foray into defensive economic nationalism.

Having leaned on the British state for survival (not for the last time), Scotland's banks could enter the fray of globalisation themselves. In two decades, they rose from the obscurity of high street branches to become one of the most controversial business clusters on the planet. RBS launched a succession of its own hostile takeovers to enter new global markets. Before the crisis, it controlled assets of £1.9 trillion, more than the UK's GDP.[6] The Scottish clearing banks, ditching their conservative reputation, bet on an ever-expanding investment bubble.

Scotland's financiers were at the vanguard of their times, reflecting a key premise of New Labour ideology, which said 'boom and bust' had been consigned to history. Scotland no longer had to apologise for its failings: it could lead the most competitive fields of world business. Scottish Labour celebrated the new buccaneering adventurism. In 2004, Scottish First Minister Jack McConnell promised to end the 'Scottish psyche that discourages risk-taking'.[7] That same year, then-RBS chief executive Fred Goodwin received a knighthood, and the commentariat lauded this exception to Scotland's safety-first, nanny-state corporatism.

Today, Goodwin stands for 'casino capitalism' and the senility of British business. Indeed, his fall exercises such imaginative sway that many attribute the whole financial bubble to his personality disorders. Gavin McCrone, former chief economist at the Scottish Office, insists 'What happened at the Royal Bank would seem to be mainly due to megalomania on the part of the chief executive, Fred Goodwin'.[8] In reality, one man's psychosis cannot destroy a company larger than many national economies unless a social order legitimises his actions.

Goodwin is a metaphor, perhaps, for comprehensive changes in the Scottish economy. Under devolution, Scotland's financial boom surpassed the rest of the UK's. The sector increased its share of Scottish GDP from 4 to 7.4 per cent, an 84 per cent rise, in the years 2000–05. This growth was far ahead of the comparative London figure (57 per cent) and RUK (25 per cent).[9] Less than 250,000 worked in Scottish manufacturing by 2006, compared to half a million in hotels and catering, and a similar amount in finance, banking and insurance. By 2008, seven of the top twenty Scottish companies were in financial services, totalling 67 per cent of turnover, 78 per cent of profit and 52 per cent of employment in top firms.[10] Scottish Development International boasted the cluster was 'second to London as a European financial location'.[11]

Once the flagship of Scotland's modernisation, today finance is the politically charged problem for any economic strategy. Its future, after the bailout and nationalisation of RBS and HBOS, is at the centre of the constitutional debate, and both sides deny complicity. For Unionists, Scottish factors explain the banks' failure; for nationalists, the blame rests with lax UK oversight and the City of London's 'casino capitalism'.

Better Together leader Alistair Darling, chancellor of the exchequer during the financial crash of 2008, explains his view:

> Despite what some suggest, the calamity which hit the Scottish banking industry wasn't imported from London but was homegrown ... when people talk about boom and bust, Scotland's bankers took up the challenge in spectacular style ... Let's remember, too, that Edinburgh's strong position in financial services depends on London's global pre-eminence in this sector.[12]

Darling makes three claims here. First, Scotland's political union with London blessed it with a financial boom. Secondly, the disaster of 2008 stemmed from risk-prone Scottish bankers, a lapse of national character. Third, the British state allowed Scotland's fallen banks to survive.

Darling's argument has an obvious flaw. The banks were *headquartered* in Scotland, but they were (de)*regulated* from Westminster, and Darling himself helped devise Blair and Brown's 'flexible' approach to the debt economy. Labour ministers pressed for 'innovation' in financial services, and urged others to repeat the formula and get filthy rich. This extended well beyond the City of London. New Labour pushed Britain's regional economies to *imitate* the London miracle, pitting urban centres in ferocious competition. This culture of deregulation encouraged Scottish banks to launch takeovers and compete as global players. By the time of the 2008 crash, just one in six RBS jobs were in Scotland. While Goodwin had ultimate responsibility, London officials made many of the riskiest investments. 'Modernisers' in New Labour, Darling among them, toured the planet proselytising about the financial miracle. His complicity in 2008 is far greater than Holyrood's combined guilt.

The growth of finance UK-wide was no accident, after all. In the last decades, financial sectors bulged relative to industry in every Western economy, but Britain's tumour was especially enormous. This reflected political decisions and an egoistic culture driven by Thatcher and built on by New Labour. Sacrificing manufacturing to a strong pound was a political choice, which, allied to deregulation of credit, benefiting finance and ruining regional economies. Finally, low wages, privatisation and council house sell-offs made people more dependent on the market. Under this stress, borrowing for week-to-week expenses, once frowned upon, became the norm. So, from having been a comparatively egalitarian society, the UK slumped to extreme inequality. The Scottish banks' crime was conforming to a long-established consensus.

But blaming the RBS/HBOS mess on the City is also mistaken. Many nationalists, Salmond and Christopher Harvie among them, attribute the crisis to South-east England's casino capitalism. This exonerates bank bosses who did untold damage to Scotland's economy, reflecting a cosy relationship between RBS and senior nationalists. Salmond himself was an RBS oil economist, while ex-RBS chief George Mathewson is a key business supporter of independence.

Scotsman columnist Lesley Riddoch goes further, blaming the crash on English individualism:

> The banking crisis could only happen in a country where cheating and deception have become institutionalised – and could only be tolerated by voters because they privately harbour hopes of rising to the same heady, rule-breaking heights themselves one day. This is the corrupting power of the American Dream and a large chunk of England has been thoroughly seduced.[13]

Both sides make this mistake of reducing economic structure to national psyche. Judging the peculiar mindset of UK capitalism is valid; but crises are system problems, not psychologies. Unlike people, systems are not good or bad, greedy or altruistic. Investor behaviour is driven by competition for new profits and markets, which rewards egoism and punishes altruism; capitalism is unstable and unjust regardless of the moral character of businesspeople. Even if we imposed psychology tests, to weed out psychopaths like Fred Goodwin from top jobs, this will not guarantee a sound economy if investment lies in private hands. Britain's particular woes derive from its global role in recent capitalist modernisation. The UK institutionalised privatisation, deregulation and free trade, all of which reshaped the English mindset.

None of these qualifications mean Scotland is doomed. Why should an independent nation repeat the UK's every error? Britain's mythmakers blame the crisis of 2008 on high government spending; they insist it was liable to hit all small economies. Denmark and Norway both kept independent currencies pegged to the euro, both had high levels of public investment, and both escaped the worst effects of recession. Many factors influenced this trajectory, but one common Nordic variable is that they withstood the temptations of deregulation and regressive taxes. Of course, independence could also open the Irish or Icelandic path, but Scotland would have greater freedom to choose. Within Westminster, we have neoliberalism or bust; or rather, neoliberalism and bust.

Globalisation

In recent Scottish history, the case of financial firms has been exceptional. As a rule, Scottish assets fell into overseas or RUK hands; and Scotland thus experienced globalisation passively, as a 'victim', although local elites were happy to profit from ceding control to multinationals.

At the start of the twentieth century, Scottish economic output was 50 per cent higher than Denmark or Norway. Soon, these nations caught up and pushed far ahead: by 1989, Scotland's GDP per capita was 89 per cent of Denmark's and 76 per cent of Norway's.[14] This occurred despite the benefits of North Sea oil. The transition to globalised capitalism has pained Scotland, and, as elsewhere, the poor suffered at the expense of upper middle classes.

Scotland was not always globalisation's casualty. A century ago, Scotland contained a self-confident and assertive business class who owned their industries. Glasgow was the 'second city of Empire' and Scotland actively globalised, as a central part of British imperialism. Much Scottish investment went overseas, and 'Scotland could be said to have been the most successfully imperialist part of Britain – excepting of course the home of finance capital in the South-East of England.'[15]

Thus, Scotland, unlike Ireland, has no history as an oppressed nation. Its economic problems resulted from the privileges, not the hardships, of Empire: they were unintended results of its earlier seniority.

Scotland's core industries and its commercial systems were built for British colonialism. Having relied on Empire, Scotland suffered an exaggerated decline. The prime causes were over-dependence on heavy engineering and overseas portfolios, which built capitalism on low wages and financial profits rather than new investments. Between 1955 and 1965, Scotland's economic performance was the worst in Western Europe.[16] By

1968, just half of Scotland's manufacturing jobs were in domestically owned plant; within a decade, the proportion was less than a third.[17] 'Scotland', noted Gavin McCrone at this time, 'is indeed suffering from a singularly British sickness.'[18]

These trends accelerated in the Thatcher and Blair eras. Only 19 per cent of large businesses (that is, over 500 employees) had Scottish headquarters by 1998.[19] In 2003, Scottish families were the main owners of just 9 of the top 100 companies; 56 were outright overseas owned.[20] Now, foreign firms control 64 per cent of employment and 78 per cent of turnover in large firms, a rise from 52 per cent and 69 per cent respectively in 2002.[21] This reflected common tendencies in world capitalism. Scotland took an exceptional course because Britain was an exceptional Empire, but other nations had similar contours.

Today, despite devolution, global corporations dictate Scotland's planning agenda. Multinationals exploit rivalries in Scottish governance, producing an anarchic development strategy. The recent public-private experiments of Edinburgh City Council are a perfect example. In response to the increasing penetration of the capital city by corporations, the Council created the Edinburgh Business Assembly (EBA). EBA, the first alliance of its type, unites councillors with companies employing over 40,000 to lobby for the 'Edinburgh interest'. It represents the largest transnational firms – including BT Scotland, Lloyds Banking Group, Standard Life and RBS – plus two universities, Scottish Enterprise, Edinburgh Council, and NHS Lothian:

> A public-private partnership unprecedented in the UK, the group gives the unabashed elite of corporate Edinburgh, plus a few other 'worthies' … a direct feed into the council's decision-making. The aim is to ensure, that on key strategic matters – transport infrastructure, business rates, Edinburgh-Glasgow collaboration – the capital's biggest employers are in step with politicians and bureaucrats.[22]

The EBA claimed to speak in the 'Edinburgh interest'. This meant the needs of big business, plus Edinburgh Council's rivalries with the Scottish Executive and other regions. In Scotland's press, the EBA muttered against dark anti-Edinburgh agendas. They resented using business tax rates, often gathered in Edinburgh, to pursue 'socialist-style redistribution' to the rest of Scotland. Since the capital is the Scottish headquarters for transnational corporations, EBA used their clout to panic the Scottish government into line. Edinburgh's residents received no consultation, and EBA excluded most local businesses.

EBA shows that big business controls more than Scottish assets. They also rule the development agenda, exploiting loopholes, trading favours and buying influence. For many decades, Scotland has reacted to losing its industries by selling itself to foreign investors, but this has not created a stable economy. Instead, companies come to Scotland for subsidies and perks, and leave when they run out, or when they find they can hire workers elsewhere for lower wages. At best, this strategy plugs gaps; but it also removes democratic levers to plan and manage resources.

The largest non-financial firms in Scotland are ex-public sector. As a candid report by RBS observed:

> Several of Scotland's major firms have a strong public sector heritage. Within the top 20 firms, the recent background of 14 could be argued to be significantly influenced by the public sector. This influence has been either directly through a privatisation (e.g. Scottish Power), or indirectly, through the liberalisation of a sector that previously had a strong public sector involvement (e.g. oil, gas and transport). One of the firms, TotalFinaElf (UK), is still partially owned by the French government, while others (e.g. British Energy, Stagecoach, First Group) continue to receive direct or indirect public subsidy for some of their activities.[23]

These corporations own core infrastructure. To change Scotland, especially in a green direction, planning between all of them will be required. But since they are privatised or 'liberalised', and they are obliged to put shareholders first, they receive cursory democratic scrutiny. This applies still more where the companies have external owners, such as Scottish Power, which is owned by the Spanish company Iberdrola.

With our key infrastructure, the interests of private owners collide with public welfare. This affects more than climate strategy. Per capita, twice as many people die in the UK as in Scandinavia from winter cold.[24] Even Siberia, with its Arctic temperatures, has lower numbers of people freezing to death. Between 2003 and 2008, the number of households in the UK in fuel poverty rose from 2 million to 4.5 million. The privatised companies that run our energy, meanwhile, gain massive dividends. Scottish Power doubled its pre-tax profits to £712 million in 2012–13 and paid an £890 million dividend to its Spanish owners, while hiking prices

7 per cent, during a recession. The Citizens Advice Bureau observes that energy profiteering forces many families 'to choose between heating and eating'. Ironically, Scottish Power sponsors conferences on fuel poverty.

Neoliberalism

For optimistic Labour leaders like Donald Dewar, devolution would provide 'Scottish solutions to Scottish problems'. But the reality was *private* solutions to Scottish problems. Holyrood presided over the further privatisation of services, the further rise of overseas ownership, growing inequalities that match most of England's, and a rightward shift in values. Any subversive potential evaporated in devolution's early years. 'The risk that the Scottish Parliament might bring democracy closer to the people and challenge vested interests has effectively been contained,' concludes sociologist David Miller. 'Market democracy under business rule has been established.'[25]

Of course, Holyrood brought benefits too. Without it, there would be no free prescription charges, the NHS would be privatised, and (Scottish) students would pay £9,000 tuition fees. Still, Scotland's Parliament drifted with steady momentum towards market-led solutions to social problems. How did this happen?

Neoliberal politics in Scotland emerged in three, overlapping stages. In the first, local and urban councils reacted to Thatcher's austerity by turning into global brands. Glasgow was the shining example of using public-private partnerships to 'regenerate' city spaces. In the second stage, under New Labour, private finance became the only potential source for investment in underfunded services. In the third, ideas themselves were privatised, as Holyrood bought in policies from the booming ecosystem of pro-market think tanks. These institutes specialise in bite-size, media-friendly prescriptions, and they enforce a conformist consensus in Holyrood.

In the 1980s, Glasgow's 'urban renaissance' pioneered market engineering. Once heralded as the second city of Empire, Scotland's industrial capital had become a byword for violence, deprivation and gloom. The severity of its environmental problems caused it to become the first city in history to deliberately try to cut its population. Under Thatcher, it thus confronted scarcities with minimal opportunities for government support. Other city councils, including Edinburgh and many in England, protested Thatcher's neglect, and tried to impose higher taxes and needs-based budgets. Glasgow took a different approach. It re-branded itself as a 'fun' retail playpark.

It got a little help from Mr Happy, whose grin adorned the slogan 'Glasgow's Miles Better'. Planners hailed the marketing campaign as a stroke of genius; it had many imitators. In keeping with the times, Glasgow civic leaders decided they would not rely on bailouts from central government. If Glasgow could shed its gloomy image, they concluded, middle-class shoppers and tourists would flood back, and Victorian-era glory would resume.

Re-branding exercises are now a routine part of governing Glasgow. All have a similar theme: the city's fun, playful, and creative side. As Law and Mooney observe:

Glasgow has become an incessant marketing campaign, emphasising art, culture and architecture, designer shopping and luxury apartments in the restored bourgeois residential quarter, the Merchant City, through to 2004's risible promotion of the city as Scotland's fashion answer to Milan: 'Glasgow: The New Black' or 'Glasgow: Scotland with Style'.[26]

The expectation was that, by waging war to replace Glasgow's gritty reputation with positive vibes, safety and niche consumerism, the city would experience an influx of shoppers, tourists and businesspeople. And by some measures the success was drastic, and its scale (putting values and morality aside) is impressive. Between 1981 and 2002, manufacturing fell from 23.2 per cent of employment in Glasgow to 7.4 per cent, while service industries rose to 87 per cent.[27] Today £2.255 billion is spent in Glasgow's shops per year as compared to £1 billion in Edinburgh.[28] Glasgow is the second city of retail in Britain, with a fashionable brand and a weak trade union movement consigned to the public sector.

Thus the World Bank commends Glasgow as a major city success story. Its redemption, after all, presents 'trickle-down economics' at the urban level, conforming to every neoliberal diktat. Supporters of this model believe that redesigning cities around rich peoples' whims provides funds to regenerate deprived areas.

But this meant exterminating negative vibes and eyesores. Glasgow's market model thus also implied an authoritarian turn. Recent urban strategies show an extraordinary hardening of attitudes to class, with police powers used to cleanse the city of anything that threatens its retail reputation. As anyone who visits Glasgow will testify, CCTV and visible policing colonise city-centre life. Geographer Gordon MacLeod calls this mix of fashionable consumption and law-and-order Glasgow's 'revanchist' urbanism.[29] The term *revanche* literally means 'revenge', and in this context refers to the violent 're-taking' of urban space by the middle classes from the working classes and democratic forces. Glasgow thus combines vigorous policing against its proletarian periphery, with an events and retail strategy to coax mobile middle-class shoppers.

Glasgow was a major success for pro-market ideas in Scotland. But its successes made no impact on social needs. Wealth has barely trickled at all: Glasgow and its fringes continue to suffer from among the most traumatic social problems in Europe. As Oxfam Scotland has noted:

> Glasgow's level and variation of income deprivation is the same as in Liverpool and Manchester. Yet Glasgow's poor health manifests in premature male mortality which is 30% higher than in these comparable cities; suicide is 70% higher; there are 32% more violent deaths; and 225% more alcohol-related deaths.[30]

A fifth of Glasgow endures child poverty, the third worst in the UK.[31] In certain wards, figures rise to 51 per cent (Springburn) and 49 per cent (Calton).[32] In Glasgow North East, more than a third of pupils left school without a single qualification in 2011, the UK's worst performance.[33] Glasgow still has severe shortages in jobs, housing and social services; health and mental illness rates are worse. None the less, the perception of renaissance lingers, and influences economic strategies far beyond Scotland. The buzzword 'place marketing' captures this phenomenon.

The second stage of neoliberal Scotland meant using the private sector to fund public projects, but this took decades of trial and error, since native forces opposed making private profit out of public services. The poll tax, although not a case of privatisation per se, was a significant case where large sections of Scotland resisted Thatcher's regressive policies. It was first launched in Scotland because indigenous Tories hoped to win back upper-middle-class Edinburgh voters. But it became a focal point for opposition, and its defeat led to Thatcher's fall.

John Major's attempts to privatise Scottish Water were also foiled by grass-roots rebellions. In 1994, the Tory proposals met 97 per cent opposition in a Strathclyde Regional Council referendum, forcing Major's government to retreat.

The construction of the Skye Bridge exposed new doubts about privatisation. This was a vanguard case of private financing for public infrastructure, with corporate investment repaid by tolls on residents. Construction began in 1992 and finished in 1995, but locals refused to pay for a public service, and launched a protest campaign, during which this sleepy part of rural Scotland saw 500 arrests. Hatred of this project forced Holyrood to bring it into public ownership in 2004, and toll collection ceased. Residents and taxpayers had paid £93.6 million for a proposal costed at £15 million.[34] The Skye Bridge example proves the Tories had uneven success in imposing privatisation schemes, since Scotland rejected their policies on instinct.

Private finance initiatives (PFIs) meant that corporations supplied capital for infrastructure, and leased it back to the public sector at the taxpayers' expense. While the formula was experimental under the Tories, under New Labour, PFI became the routine response to any project. Officially, PFI was a last resort when public funding proved too expensive, but in practice this was not the case. 'When there is a limited amount of public-sector capital, as there is … it's PFI or bust,' admitted former health secretary Alan Milburn in 1997.[35] For Holyrood, it maintained a fiction of 'Scottish solutions to Scottish problems'. In reality, it produced fat profits and thinly disguised debt. 'PFIs have always been the NHS's Plan A for building new hospitals … There never was a Plan B,' explained Labour Health Secretary Alan Johnson in 2009.[36]

By the close of Labour's reign, they had accrued £260 billion of PFI commitments for investments worth £60 billion. Notorious projects include Edinburgh's new Royal Infirmary, priced at £148 million and run by a firm called Consort, which cost taxpayers £1.26 billion.[37] Professionals condemned its shoddy design and safety failings. At one stage, the PFI contractors unexpectedly shut off the power to the hospital, and surgeons had to keep a patient alive by torchlight, after an electricity blackout hit heart monitors and breathing machines. After another power failure, 'an expectant father had to use the torch app on his smartphone to find his newborn son in a birthing pool when the lights failed last December.'[38] Consort also neglected to inform staff when fire alarms and panic alarms crashed.

PFI has been a boon for private firms. Primary PFI investors make an *average profit* of 50 per cent, according to a House of Commons report, compared to a profit margin of 2 or 3 per cent on ordinary construction projects.[39] For taxpayers, they have been a costly disaster. As another Commons report notes, 'PFI projects are significantly more expensive to fund over the life of a project ... in some areas PFI seems to perform more poorly ... PFI is also inherently inflexible, especially for NHS projects.'[40] Also, as the Infirmary case shows, PFIs often put life-and-death decisions in the hands of bungling contractors.

Jack McConnell's Labour administration backed PFI without any questions. McConnell argued:

> For too long Scottish politics has been dominated by a consensus that public services came before enterprise and growth. That enterprise was even something to be ashamed of or embarrassed about. Scottish Labour must embrace enterprise. We must be the party of enterprise because a dynamic economy means opportunities for Scots and resources for schools and hospitals.[41]

McConnell's own trajectory says a lot about the corporate domination of Holyrood. In the early years of New Labour, he worked with the lobbying arm of Beattie Media, a PR agency. In a candid interview with an undercover reporter from the *Observer*, the lobbyists said they 'appointed Jack McConnell ... in the certain knowledge that Jack would get a safe seat from the Labour Party, and in the hope and expectation that he would also get a cabinet position within the new administration'.[42]

The lobbyists also claimed to influence McConnell's diary and gain easy access for clients. Another leading figure in the affair was Kevin Reid, son of Labour's John, who worked for Labour before joining Beattie. He boasted: 'I know the secretary of state very, very well because he's my father.'[43] In 1991, this web expanded into the 'lobbygate scandal'. McConnell testified about his corporate links before the Parliamentary Standards Committee. Although he denied wrongdoing, the debacle disclosed how quickly Holyrood officials became corporate puppets. A light touch on the regulation of standards was normalised. As the *Daily Record* observed, the committee's 'kid gloves handling of McConnell was not so much a grilling as a gentle toasting'.[44] This was the context for McConnell's impatience with critics of the market.

The final stage of market hegemony in Scotland was the rise of think tanks. Across the world, neoliberal ideas were spread by semi-official advisers and experts trained in neoclassical economic dogma. For Thatcher,

Reagan, Pinochet and other vanguard neoliberals, the destruction of any hint of leftish ideologies was a key goal in the class war. Hence, she railed against liberal academics, as well as Keynesian-inspired development agencies in Scotland:

> Perceiving the academic establishment to be arrayed on a spectrum from left-liberal to socialist, the Conservative government now turned for advice to individuals associated with the Institute of Economic Affairs and the Adam Smith Institute. Think tanks and external advisers became a fixture in public administration, cutting out academic economists and diminishing their authority.[45]

The proliferation of think tanks, which bypass stipulations of impartial knowledge, has been a key feature of neoliberalism worldwide. These bodies flourished after devolution. Almost all of them have a Third Way or outright neoliberal ideology, and very few engage with independence: only the Jimmy Reid Foundation flouts this rule. Think tanks depend on corporate donations for survival, and thus every large institute in Scotland has a roster of sponsors from the top corporations: BT Scotland, RBS, HBOS, and so on.

Although think tanks try to bypass the formal rules of university knowledge, they are changing the way universities think. Many think tanks are connected to leading academics or, in many cases, to whole faculties. The David Hume Institute, a right-wing institute, is an extension of Edinburgh University, for instance. They specialise in 'Easy Academia', light-weight bite-size factoids and nifty policy titbits. They supply an intellectual meeting ground between elements of the Scottish elite: New Club denizens, professors, journalists, businesspeople, lobbyists and politicians.

The case of think tanks shows corporate Scotland has colonised more than property. Ideas have been privatised as well. The link between knowledge and policy is no longer guided by strict rules, and just as contractors profit from building projects, so markets conducted hostile takeovers on ideas. Of course, academic elitism is not itself a virtue; and more grass-roots input would improve Holyrood services. But instead, the breakdown in standards is thoroughly dominated by amateurish neoliberal elites, schooled in the conformist bromides of global capitalism.

Conclusion

This chapter gives just a flavour of corporate dominance in Scotland. To achieve full independence, we must measure the scale of their influence and the scope of their power. Unless the financial sector is democratised, Scotland's investment strategy will be anarchic and oriented towards short-term profits. Unless we confront external ownership, it will be difficult to use our resources to meet the challenges of poverty and the green revolution. Unless we address the colonisation of policy and ideas by the market, we will repeat all the same mistakes as New Labour. An effective independence must combat these influences, or get caught in the global race to the bottom, just like Britain.

Supporters of independence face a dilemma. They insist that an independent Scotland would have a 'stable' economy, attractive to global business and a world leader in innovation, but they also see independence as a means to eradicate poverty and promote equality for all citizens. Of course, many small countries in Northern Europe manage to be far more equal than Scotland, and to sustain a higher standard of economic development in general. But how can Scotland take the first steps towards this Nordic model?

One option is a version of trickle-down economics. Since an independent Scotland could avoid inefficiency at the top, they argue, it will give greater opportunities lower down. It follows that cutting corporation tax in half would help eradicate poverty and inequality. Many small countries have tried this path; their gravestones litter European capitalism, from Iceland to Ireland to Greece to Latvia.

Others deny the dilemma. Since an independent Scotland would not spend money on wasteful products like Trident and aggressive wars, it could free up resources to build an equal society and a vigorous market economy at once. A Yes vote would improve things regardless of what we do with it. We have tried to show the dangers of these views; their worthy optimism does not confront private interests and conflicts resulting from Scotland's capitalist structure.

A third formula says that a fundamental redistribution of income in Scotland, from rich to poor, would create a more efficient capitalist economy. This is the only economic case for independence to gain serious academic endorsement. Indeed, the most significant development expert in the world, Professor Joseph Stiglitz, urges Scotland to follow this path.

Stiglitz is not only a Nobel Prize-winning economist; he is also (rare in his profession) a public intellectual with a global audience.

Like Keynes, he is an unorthodox establishment critic who wants to save markets from their flaws. His verdict on the British economy is damning. His reasoning, backed up by statistics, is that market systems with high rates of inequality grow slower than equal societies. Since 1975, the income gap in Britain has grown faster than in any other developed nation, and this trajectory seems to have no limits. The likelihood is thus stunted prospects for Britain, for the foreseeable future, unless Scotland moves towards greater autonomy, fast.

This is the best possible endorsement for the Yes case. Stiglitz is a titan of his field, a former chief economist of the World Bank and arguably the most famous authority in economic policy in the world today. No academic of equal stature has endorsed either side of the 2014 debate. But Yes officials are very reluctant to mention him, even when their economic credibility is under attack. Why have they been so bashful?

The reason, we suspect, is that Yes Scotland are aware of something that seems to escape Stiglitz's attention. Assuming Stiglitz's calculations are correct, and more equal capitalisms are better for everyone, we must still convince Scottish elites to freely surrender their existing privileges. Without coercion, would they submit to the 'common good'?

The UK gives Scottish big business and landowners the best deal in Europe. They get an authoritarian hand over trade unions, low taxes and generous subsidies. They fear any change, and hence view independence as jeopardising their interests. Indeed, seeing themselves as global and mobile, they are preparing already to remove their assets from Scotland if their privileges are imperilled. Unless we apprehend Scotland's real rulers, the 2014 case remains intellectually stagnant and conformist, and arguing for a just and equal society gets lost in euphemisms.

These are not reasons to fear independence. Scots flinched from home rule in 1979 because they believed ominous economic forecasts from the British media; the result was a decade of torment under Thatcher. In the current context, Scotland is almost guaranteed more of this, with all UK parties committed to austerity. The power of ruling elites and global corporations is hardly unique to Scotland's economy. Independence would at least give us the powers and the democratic channels to build defences, which we lack at present under Westminster.

In 1975, sociologists Scott and Hughes wrote, 'The success of a socialist strategy for Scotland depends upon its being able to counter the economic power of the upper class in Scotland and its links with international capital.'[46] This remains true today, but things have changed. Global corporations adopted new tactics to evade democratic controls, in both factories and parliaments. While the Left in Scotland, broadly conceived, succeeded in resisting the more obscene intrusions like the poll tax, NHS privatisation, and £9,000 student fees, neoliberal values have taken institutional form. Scotland's income inequality, measured by the GINI coefficient, reached parity with England under devolution, and our economic and social structure resembles RUK and even the US, rather than the Nordic countries. Only concerted resistance, and coercion against Scotland's rulers, can change this path.

The question of political agency is paramount. An alternative path might be desirable and workable, but cold economic interest often prevails over reason and logic. Large parts of Scotland have vested interests in the present order, and they will fight independence until the last; if they lose, they will fight to keep their privileges under independence. Opposing the British state without countering neoliberalism in Holyrood is flawed. At present, no mainstream Holyrood party commits to redistributing wealth. Although explicitly capitalist parties have vanished, this does pose problems. The SNP and Labour express concern for 'social justice', but in practice impose market solutions, providing an adequate channel for corporate power. Whatever happens in 2014, Scotland needs a bigger, broader platform to oppose Caledonia PLC.

4

Alliances and Divisions: Scottish Politics in the Holyrood Era

In 2004, a *Scotsman* article appeared under the headline: 'We've never had it so good.'[1] It quoted Edinburgh University sociologists David McCrone, Lindsay Paterson and Frank Bechhofer, saying that Scotland had become 'a more affluent, comfortable and pleasant place'. Poverty remained, they conceded, and perhaps it was 'more scandalous because of the surrounding affluence'. Even so, after Thatcher and New Labour, Scotland was an upwardly mobile society, dominated by middle-class professionals, resembling the rest of the UK. 'A society dominated neither by primary or secondary producers, nor by manual jobs, is not, on the whole, a working class society', they argue.[2] So Scotland's non-conformity to the Westminster consensus becomes a puzzle. On two fronts, Scotland diverges: professing communitarian values, despite its yuppie realities, and supporting more home rule, despite fusing in practice with UK capitalism.

To reconcile these seeming contradictions, several qualifications must be made. The notion of a homogenous professional society, modified by a residue of poverty, fails to capture social divisions. Scotland's so-called 'professional' and 'service' classes are tricky categories, covering a swathe of occupations and incomes, from low-paid teachers and hairdressers to bankers and engineers. Just 13 per cent of Scotland's employed earns a salary more than £34,000. McCrone, Paterson and Bechhofer say little in their work about Scotland's elites, the top families who earn hundreds of times more than the poorest. Nor do they cover in depth the de-skilling of white-collar jobs.

Instead, they interpret recent changes as a dichotomy: Scottish communitarian values versus the real curve of social change. But if we understand that Scotland's so-called middle class is scattered and divided, this contradiction vanishes. Collectivist values become more than romantic throwbacks to the industrial era and Calvinism. They stand for real differences about Scotland's unequal distribution of wealth and income, today.

The Edinburgh sociologists do not assess politics in the rest of Britain, despite implying the contrast with Scotland. Perhaps the true task, rather than hunting for the roots of Scottish deviance, should be dissecting Westminster's eccentricity. The peculiarities of electing the House of Commons, and the patronage system that dominates the Lords, shape Britain's political geography. The real contrast is between most British people, with economic interests in collectivism, and the Westminster consensus, which frames elections around immigration, Europe and crime. Scotland, with two competing moderate parties, is not a leftist curiosity; Westminster, with three authoritarian neoliberal parties, is unusually reactionary. The gravity of UK politics, though, does pull Scottish ideas to the right, impeding a proper debate about social divisions.

Westminster serves as a right-wing drag for two reasons. One is the united front between the commanding heights of British business and the Tory Party, which receives half of its donations from bankers and financiers alone (see Chapter 1). This has allowed a party with an out-of-touch membership, averaging 68 years old, to stay electable.[3]

The second problem is 'middle England', the imagined idyll that dominates Westminster electoral thinking. Middle England, composed of 'hard-working families', is individualist in economic terms, and conformist in everything else. Opportunity plus stability is the formula: lower taxes and privatisation, without threatening the white, heterosexual status quo. The Commons consensus cannot tolerate deviation from these values.

Middle England is both a mythological beast and a real entity. The term 'middle' is deceptive, since 66 per cent of Britain earn below the national mean, while just 7 per cent pay the top rate of tax.[4] Moreover, Britain's workforce became *less* white, heterosexual and male-dominated, while politicians took greater pains to pander to family values and suburban mores. Westminster reacted to a tabloid backlash against feminism and multiculturalism by throwing a conformist blanket over political debate.

As the UK returned to Victorian-era inequalities, there were real ideological shifts, reshaping English values but altering Britain as a whole. The buzzword was 'aspiration'. While white-collar workers had to accept proletarian pay and conditions, they clung more than ever to petty-bourgeois status. A new consumerism emerged, driven by credit cards and mortgages rather than rising wages, along with a new authoritarian bigotry against 'chavs' and 'neds'. Before 2008, Moneysupermarket.com noted 6 million 'wannabe middle-class' UK households on annual salaries of *less than £15,000* sustaining weekly incomes with bank loans and plastic debt.[5] The New Labour generation built economic growth on false expectations of prosperity and fears about falling into the criminal underclass.

Future historians might speculate that Middle Britain was a product of Blairite spin. Many commentators question its stamina in the crisis era, where aspirational urges conflict with the mood of austerity. Ed Miliband modified its nuances, speaking instead of the 'squeezed middle'. Beneath this, though, was a hardening of authoritarian rhetoric against immigration. Even if Miliband recognises that egoism has not benefited all of Britain, he has not broken from Middle England's white conformism. And we can measure the power of the Middle Britain idea by examining shifting views of the Labour Party. In 1987, many people (46 per cent) still felt Labour very closely looked after working-class interests. By 2005, this had fallen to just 10 per cent.[6]

Fear of Middle Britain's revenge, together with the strength of the Tories, drags Westminster Labour to the right. Two factors make changing this direction difficult. The first-past-the-post election system means that a few swing constituencies are the pivot of election strategy. Thus, the battle is to turn upper-middle-class Tory voters to Labour, a zero-sum game, rather than to raise working-class participation. The result is that a small fraction of Britain decides elections in practice. The major irony of British politics is that Blair achieved massive majorities (for example, in 2001) with far less votes than Kinnock received in his 1992 defeat.[7] Behind this was a plummeting Tory vote, and the absurdities of the UK's electoral arithmetic.

The absence of a parliamentary choice to Labour's Left exacerbates these problems. Other parties lack the financial muscle to compete with the Westminster mainstream. A few candidates have broken this rule, but whether George Galloway MP (Respect) and Caroline Lucas MP (Green Party) can build on their success is debatable.

These conditions leave Holyrood Labour little room for manoeuvre, and the UK party allows sparse openings for autonomy. Labour's feelers are tuned to Middle Britain, as they continue to confront the Tories by the method of 'triangulation'.

Labour Hegemony?

For many years, Labour's grass roots contested this path, and Blair could not declare hegemony in Scotland. Before devolution, there was a 'small 'n' nationalist' camp in Labour who spoke of politics with an independent Scottish dimension. Leftist sentiment in Scotland has often inclined this way, while the right and the London-oriented union bureaucracy have tended towards centralism. Scottish Labour Action (SLA), a pluralist left group involving Dennis Canavan, John McAllion, Susan Deacon and others, championed this post-tribal politics. An SLA pamphlet warned of the dangers Labour faced by imposing Westminster-style neoliberalism: 'If the party does not devolve and is seen as having its Scottish policy run from London, it will put itself at a considerable disadvantage compared to its competitors. In time, the Scottish people will want their parties home grown, and Labour will have to change or leave the political stage to others.'[8]

Opposing this was a shadowy Blairite cabal known as 'the Network'. Right-wing fixers such as Jim Murphy and ambitious centrists such as Jack McConnell led this faction, allied with a supporting cast of trade union officials inclined towards London central offices. The Network's aim was simple: to scour Labour of ideas and people linked to 'soft nationalism' and 'Old Labour'. Devolution, they insisted, should not disturb Blair's wooing of Middle Britain, and would not be a bridge back to social democracy.

Two showdowns disclosed these schisms. One dispute concerned Blair's proposal for an additional question in the devolution referendum, about whether the new Parliament could raise taxes. Blair was keen to dismiss any notion of using Holyrood for social change. Tax-raising powers, he insisted, would not surpass 'the smallest English parish council'. 'Sovereignty', he said in a 1997 *Scotsman* interview, 'rests with me as an English MP and that's the way it will stay.'[9]

A second dispute surfaced over how to choose candidates, with Blairite loyalists trying to stage-manage proceedings. 'The selection process is about high standards, a proven commitment to the Labour Party and, firmly, a non-flirtation with other parties,' said one of the panel.[10] 'They have to be able to demonstrate commitment and loyalty to the party.' By 'the party', they meant 'New' Labour, and this meant Blair.

Labour was thus putting up tribal shutters. They dreaded the power of a good example in Holyrood, of working relations among a broad sector of the Left. To avoid this, the Network aimed to wrest control of Labour's Scottish Executive Committee; and they succeeded, wiping out the last elements of Leftism in a few years. Although not every ploy was successful, the trend was clear. Blairite loyalists moved to block sitting MP Dennis Canavan from standing as a Labour candidate in Falkirk. Alas for them, he secured the election as a left-wing independent. Canavan got his revenge, but many others were bullied out, or found their positions untenable as the party flaunted its yuppie credentials.

For Blairites, total victory in Scotland was hard won, and a few leftist and even pro-independence figures escaped the cull. The press referred to MSPs John McAllion, Cathy Jamieson and (ironically, in retrospect) Johann Lamont as a tax-raising 'left faction'.[11] In a concession to party unity, Donald Dewar gave McAllion a role on the front bench. But within a few years, this group had either resigned in disgust, or had drunk New Labour's Kool Aid.

The Iraq War debate proved a watershed. Six Labour MSPs rebelled against the party in a Holyrood vote: Bill Butler, Susan Deacon, Cathy Peattie, McAllion, Pauline McNeill and Elaine Smith. Soon after, Malcolm Chisholm expressed regret at voting for the war. These honourable exceptions aside, Iraq served to prove Scottish Labour's docility. Six MSPs was a small fraction of Holyrood Labour. By contrast, 139 Labour MPs, close to a third, defied Blair in the compliant ranks of Westminster, despite enormous pressure. In Holyrood, the percentage of dissenting MSPs was 10 per cent, even though it was easier to oppose war, since their vote had no practical impact. Nevertheless, they stood firm and loyal behind Blair's backing for Bush, to prevent a victory for the anti-war parties.

This was the point where Labour support started to atrophy. In 2003, the number of Labour MSPs fell from 56 to 50. Labour haemorrhaged trust over its open alliance with the US neocons, and it has never returned. In later elections, their share fell to 46 and then 37 seats.

Labour has continued to drift rightwards across parliaments. Two factors explain this: the Blairite purge against the Left in the early years of devolution, and the pressure of UK-wide party unity. Responding to this, a remarkable cleavage opened between right-wing policies and professed socialist values. Tribal loyalties meant few dissented from

UK neoliberalism. But the more Scottish Labour calls for draconian pro-market reforms, the more they throw around phrases like 'social justice', 'working-class communities' and even 'socialism'.

The result is authoritarian populism, combining tough talk and communitarian values. Justifying her stance on policing, Cathy Jamieson, once seen as a figure of the Left, defended her views in Old Labour terms. 'There is nothing left wing or socialist about allowing our communities to be terrorised by youths who do things like break off railings to use as weapons or hide knives in bushes to pick up later,' she retorted.[12] Holyrood Labour appeals to the old distinction between respectable and rough working classes. Thus, Duncan McNeill MSP made a passionate defence of his right to label young people 'neds': 'What are we supposed to call them – the guys that hang about the streets? Tracksuit ambassadors? Shoplifters as retail stock relocation operatives? Drug dealers as independent pharmaceutical consultants? What are we to call them?'[13]

McConnell's bill on anti-social behaviour nodded in this direction. 'Although they may be completely innocent of any crime or offence', it noted, 'the presence of any group of young people can be seen as intimidating and contribute to fear of crime.'[14] But, as Jamieson hints, they saw this hard talk as harmonious with socialist values. The further Labour drifted to the right, the more they would rail against nationalism and the more they would stress how much they 'listened' to working-class communities.

So when the neoliberal moderniser Wendy Alexander became leader, she said the battle in Scotland was between 'socialism' (that is, her views) and 'nationalism' (the SNP). The irony, remarked Elaine Smith, chair of the Scottish Campaign for Socialism in the Labour Party, was that the SNP backed socialist policies opposed by Labour: ending council houses sales, for instance, and free prescriptions.[15]

McConnell, as Labour leader, prioritised 'public service modernisation' and creating a 'culture of entrepreneurship'. This plea for more private-sector involvement in Scottish life is a neoliberal commonplace, but McConnell pitched his appeal in terms of 'socialism', 'haves-and-have-nots' and 'egalitarian Scotland'. Recalling his 'very ordinary background', he insisted his reforms were 'not some secret plot to implement Thatcherism by the back door, or an attempt to divert attention from the substance through style'.[16]

Recently, Johann Lamont derided Scotland's 'something for nothing culture', and spoke for abolishing free personal care for the elderly, free prescriptions and free education. Later, she called for a cuts commission to trim Holyrood budgets. When Douglas Alexander defended Lamont's attacks on universal benefits, he quoted Nye Bevan: 'The religion of socialism is the language of priorities.'[17]

Thus, the Scottish Labour Party expresses pride in their working-class roots, real or romanticised. They continue to profess concern for the poor, and to deride the SNP's 'elitism'. They wear a fig-leaf of sentimental socialist values. Scottish Labour has not morphed into Blairism, they insist, because they still listen to people in council estates, and care about their plight.

In reality, they are the party of middle Scotland, appealing to a conformist, authoritarian streak, while making fitful appeals to leftist loyalties with attacks on 'Tartan Tories'. All of this reflected its changing socio-economic profile. One by one, Holyrood Labour lost its most loyal constituencies. For all their moralism about 'communities', they often look like the most electable right-wing alternative to the SNP. Still, due to the peculiarities of British politics, they are bankrolled by the trade union movement. This lack of social and ideological fit between party bases, voters and policies makes Holyrood alliances unsustainable.

Tartan Tories?

Very few commentators correctly predicted the 2011 election result. The SNP, defying opinion polls going back a year, beat Labour to achieve an unprecedented overall majority, thanks to a large swing in working-class sentiment. 'Labour's vote … fell more heavily in areas with more working class voters,' observed Professor John Curtice, 'and in areas with relatively high levels of social deprivation.'[18] Further research has shown that 36 per cent of working-class people voted Labour, compared to 42 per cent for the SNP.

The SNP dominated the Irish Catholic vote, bucking the historical link between this group and Labour.[19] It reflected a trend, with Labour's core constituencies deserting the party. In 2003, Muslims switched allegiance en masse from Labour to the SNP in protest against war in Iraq. The SNP has thus captured parts of Labour's traditional heartlands, and cannot be reduced to a yuppie party. Commentators disagree on interpretations of this shift. One academic suggests, 'That a visible and cultural minority should switch their votes to the local nationalist party is a remarkable endorsement of the SNP's claim to have embraced a multicultural vision of the nation.'[20] Perhaps; but it may just show repulsion at Labour's chauvinist turn.

In policy terms, as opposed to professed values, the SNP acts on more progressive terms than Labour. This applies on a range of issues from troops in Iraq and nukes on the Clyde, to universal benefits, local income taxes and council housing. Indeed, Labour is rarely outright to the left of the SNP on any issue. One exception is that the SNP backs low corporation tax, although this would only apply after independence. On occasion, Labour plays to the Left on gender, but like their other professions to socialist values, this barely expresses itself in outright policy disagreements.

The SNP is by no means a radical party. Privatised bus kingpin Brian Souter, notorious for his campaign to stop schools 'teaching' homosexuality, bankrolled Salmond's 2011 election. In terms of class affiliation, its members appear slightly to the right of Labour. A 1997 survey showed that, of Labour members who identify with a class, 73 per cent say working class.[21] By contrast, SNP members, in a survey in 2007–08, were far less likely to put themselves in a class. Where they did, 46 per cent said working class, next to 54 per cent middle class.[22] Of course, in the decade between these polls, Scottish Labour lurched to the right, which may cause differences to narrow. But we might still expect Labour to maintain a stronger working-class identity.

The picture becomes more mixed in terms of objective class status. Eighteen per cent of Scottish Labour members are working class, as of 1997, according to Goldthorpe's occupational classification. This is quite a bit higher than the SNP as of 2007–08 (10 per cent). But a similar number belong to the top grade of salary-earners: both parties are dominated by this group, which forms 61 per cent of SNP and 59 per cent of Labour. Also, a much higher rate of SNP members are employed in routine non-manual jobs (17 per cent) than Labour (12 per cent).[23] Another major difference is that more SNP members, compared to Labour, work in the private sector.

A similar ambiguous pattern emerges if we measure class by income. As James Mitchell and colleagues note:

> The overall distribution of incomes in the SNP ... looks similar to that in other parties. However, four in ten members are retired and likely to have incomes significantly below what they would have earned in real terms prior to retirement. When retired members are excluded ... the average household income rises to between £30,000 and £40,000 from between £20,000 and £30,000.[24]

Measured by political values, 57 per cent of active members of the SNP see their party as left-wing. Most SNP members, moreover, believe they are to the left of Labour. Those who joined the SNP during the Thatcher era are the most prone to these views, with 71 per cent of this group considering Labour right-wing.[25] This is a subjective measure and we should be wary of reaching hasty conclusions, but to a degree it reflects reality. If we measure by voting patterns, the result is similar. As of 1997, left-wing Scots were as likely to vote SNP as Labour.[26] By 2003, voters viewed the SNP as Scotland's progressive party.[27] Detecting Scottish ideological differences, on a left–right scale, is thus messy. But on policy, the SNP normally pitches to Labour's left; on international issues, they consistently outflank Labour from the left, in values and in practice.

There are anomalies, of course. For instance, research has shown that on-the-street SNP voters (as opposed to members) were sometimes more likely to take chauvinist lines on racism. Holyrood Labour avoids UK-style racialised politics; Jack McConnell, for example, refused to back the crackdown on asylum seekers in Dungavel detention centre. This reflects one area where Scottish Labour clearly improved over their UK counterparts. Although Scots may still have racist views, they do not enter the sphere of electoral competition. This contributes to a smaller rate of racial violence, since politicians do not legitimise hatred. Thus, in the three weeks after the London bombings in 2005, London police reported a 600 per cent rise in incidents involving race hate, next to 20 per cent in Scotland.[28]

Labour voters are not always right-wing by instincts, even compared to the SNP, and Scotland's loyalties are complex and fractured. Neither party conforms to the wishes of its core supporters; in particular, trying to explain their behaviour by who funds them often verges on the ridiculous. One major difference is that the SNP has vital room for tactical manoeuvre, since Holyrood politics defines its strategy. By contrast, Scottish Labour drags Middle England around like a ball and chain. Both parties are divided in many directions: by memberships, by their electoral constituencies, by their financial links, by momentary tactical expediency.

The SNP's internal divisions revolve around two axes: left versus right, and gradualist versus 'fundamentalist'. But there are overlaps between these sides, as left-wing members are far more likely to take a so-called fundamentalist line on independence. The neoliberal right, led by Michael Russell, tends to favour accommodating to the mainstream and establishing a good reputation for managing the current settlement. Their guidelines are not always neat: there are left-wing figures, for example, Nicola Sturgeon, who have been won to gradualism.

The right in the SNP often goes further than Labour in its pro-market ideas. Russell penned an extraordinary book, *Grasping the Thistle*, calling for Scotland to carry out massive cuts to the public sector.[29] Scotland, for Russell, should aim to compete with the low-wage economies of India and China; indeed, he argued that Scotland should replicate their minimal welfare systems. Even the most right-wing Scottish Labour figures, such as Tom Harris and Jim Murphy, would not go this far in public.

Salmond came of age in the left-wing 79 Group, and took many years to abandon his 'fundamentalist' views on constitutional matters. Since returning to the Scottish Parliament, he has re-branded himself, praising Thatcher and positioning himself as a moderate. He has gained the friendship and endorsement of a whole series of unsavoury characters, from Brian Souter to Rupert Murdoch and ex Rangers chairman Sir David Murray.

However, the left of the SNP are often far more radical than 'Old Labour'. The SNP elect mainstream politicians who call for abolishing the monarchy, tax-and-spend policies, and re-nationalisation. Anti-war and anti-Trident views are taken as party policy, although they lapsed over Afghanistan and the Falklands. The language of anti-imperialism is common: elected SNP officials are happy to call Tony Blair a 'war criminal'.

Tensions are surfacing within the SNP, despite recent electoral successes. As we will examine in the next chapter, there has been a meek and moderate approach to independence, which alienates large parts of the membership. A key moment was the vote at the 2012 SNP Conference on whether to abandon opposition to the US-led nuclear NATO alliance. The right and gradualists hoped that abandoning this view would make the Yes case credible. Leaders exerted intense pressure on party members, warning of dire consequences if they defied this command. The left showed its autonomy by mobilising a strong rebellion. The result was a vote of 426 to 332 in favour of NATO, a creditable showcase for the autonomy of the nationalist Left.

NATO exposed a major dilemma between protest and power. Detectable divisions have emerged between those stressing the need for a break with the British state, and moderates intent on developing a reputation for service-provision. At present, gradualists stay in control, In particular over Yes campaign strategy. Whether their minimal platform will convince people to vote Yes may be debated. If it fails, new conflicts will arise about the purpose of Scottish nationalism.

Unionism Today

Before considering Yes Scotland in the next chapter, their opponents deserve some consideration. Better Together is, at first glance, a curious alliance. It is composed of all the Westminster parties, who are otherwise battling against each other. But its parts have very harmonious working relations, and there have been few signs of internal discord.

Scottish Labour's approach to Better Together conflicts with its usual tribal politics. In any other matter since devolution, they have fought vicious turf wars, especially with the broader Left and the SNP. Labour officials spurn any opportunity for joint campaigning with nationalists over issues like the 'bedroom tax'. But when the safety of the Union is imperilled, Labour puts aside any differences (real or imagined) between their own politics and the Con-Dem agenda. David Cameron, Nick Clegg, Tony Blair and every brand of militarist are acceptable allies. This show of unity reveals a great deal about Labour's core commitments.

A key test emerged when Better Together released their list of donors. The vast bulk of their campaign funding, it showed, came from Ian Taylor, an oil dealer and key Tory backer, who pledged £500,000.[30] Taylor was implicated in the 'cash for access' scandal, after his company, Vitol, received government help to set up a Libyan oil deal. Vitol is also reported to have paid massive bribes to the fascist Serbian warlord Arkan, who faced indictment at The Hague for 'wilfully causing great suffering, cruel treatment, murder, wilful killing, rape, and other inhumane acts'. In a US court, Vitol pleaded guilty to grand larceny for providing paybacks to the national oil company in Saddam Hussein's Iraq, and had to pay $17.5 million in fines.[31]

Before the Better Together donation scandal, Labour MP John Mann called on the Tories to return Taylor's cash. 'Vitol was accused of "immoral" trade and "backing corrupt regimes",' he said, and Taylor's 'dirty money' should be sent back.[32] Douglas Alexander MP also criticised Taylor's donations to the Tories. But once Labour joined Better Together, they had no compunctions about accepting the donation. 'Ian Taylor is a respected figure internationally, in the UK and in Scotland,' they said in a statement.

'He has a long history of philanthropy and his personal investment has revived the Harris Tweed industry in Scotland.'[33]

The Taylor scandal took a nasty turn when Better Together sent in high-powered lawyers against the National Collective website, after a student published a story exposing Taylor's malfeasance.[34] It was a revealing battle. A team of volunteers, most of them under age 30, ran National Collective, which tried to promote independence through the arts. Better Together is an alliance of the most powerful Westminster parties, funded by big-business donors who the parties protect at all costs.

With Labour trying ever harder to distance itself from its trade unions, Better Together feels like an odd glimpse into the future. It is to the right of Yes Scotland on every issue, and its agenda has consisted in using elite media contacts to plant scare stories. While Yes Scotland has a grass-roots support base, and independent groups to the left of it including National Collective and the Radical Independence Campaign, the unionist camp is composed of big business and upper-class networks. It hints at what an allied Westminster will look like without the element of trade unions.

Since devolution, Scotland has lived in less fear of the Tories. The anomaly of Holyrood today, versus Westminster, is the absence of a party with big business or landed personnel. But Better Together warns of an emerging right-wing in Scotland. The alliance's politics have received little scrutiny, and its internal differences are not often exposed. It represents a fully consistent and complementary alliance of British nationalists, with no visible tensions. A strong No vote in 2014 could open new opportunities for this united front, allowing a new right to emerge in a hopeless vacuum.

5

Yes We Can, But We Need to Change: Strategy and 2014

In 2011, Salmond's SNP looked invincible. After trailing Scottish Labour in polls for a year, they somehow managed an overwhelming victory in the Holyrood elections. This confounded media predictions, and exposed the fragility of devolved institutions, which were designed to make a nationalist majority impossible. After achieving a miracle, the faithful wanted the next step, to achieve the party's stated aim: full independence. Surveys showed public opinion was warming to the idea, and a clear majority endorsed shifting most fiscal powers to Holyrood. With momentum behind them, convincing Scotland to back full autonomy seemed a small task.

All that remained were details – the how, when and what of voting – but here, having looked unassailable, Salmond faltered. He hesitated over naming the referendum date, and fretted over putting 'devolution max' – that is, total fiscal autonomy – on the ballot. Weak leadership handed the initiative to Cameron's Con-Dem coalition, who used the media to slow momentum towards independence by niggling over the small print.

Having reached a compromise, underlying confusions spilled over into a bungled opening for the campaign designed to win a Yes vote.[1] From the beginning, the SNP mishandled Yes Scotland. The launch itself sent the wrong message, with not a single ethnic minority, and just one woman, appearing on the platform of ten speakers. This did not look like a higher form of democracy; indeed, even supporters like Lesley Riddoch noted its uncanny affinity with Westminster elitism.[2] Salmond promised the 'biggest grass-roots campaign in Scottish history', a worthy aim, but the event itself felt staid and conformist, and looked like a mass of grey suits.

Since this stuttering launch, support for a Yes vote has never moved near a majority – indeed, has sometimes fallen to historic lows. The official campaign has been lifeless, dithering over clear opportunities and tempering change in cautious platitudes. True, inept leadership did not cause the 'patriotic' surge after the Olympics, Will and Kate's marriage, and the Royal baby, but Scots' fondness for flag-waving spectacles does not explain weak polls. Also true, Scottish and British media are biased against independence; but who expected value-free critical insight from the *Mail*? Neither kitschy festivities nor a fanatical unionist press explains why many Scots are willing to countenance a No vote.

Differences over strategy are not always explainable in strict left-versus-right terms, and we are not just advocating a caricatured 'leftist turn'. The Yes Scotland board represents socialists as well as entrepreneurs and dignitaries, but these leaders have little say on the message itself. Campaign officials sell the basics of independence and build networks, but without setting agendas; the power to define 2014's content lies with Salmond's leadership. Only the SNP can commit Scotland to NATO at party conferences, while reiterating, with painful regularity, that 'Scotland's people have the final say' over post-independence institutions.

When Yes Scotland chair Dennis Canavan calls for abolishing the monarchy, everybody knows he speaks for himself, not for the campaign he figureheads. Internal SNP decisions bind the campaign and set agendas, which is why global diplomats swarm around their 2013 conference, not Yes Scotland caucuses. SNP managers handpicked the campaign's board from existing contacts, and two SNP members, Angus Robertson and Stephen Noon, handled its early strategy. The former is an MP on the militarist wing of the party; the latter is a 'Jesuit educated former Young Conservative.'[3] Although left-leaning Nicola Sturgeon replaced the unpopular Robertson, Yes Scotland's guiding philosophy stayed intact.

The SNP must balance stabilising their Holyrood majority, and convincing Scotland to break the British state. The latter requires riskier strategies and more radical arguments, both of which expose Salmond's government. A truce emerged between these priorities, whereby independence campaigning would remain within safe boundaries, without compromising SNP hegemony.

As of 2013, many look at dismal polls and dismiss any chance of independence, but we take a different view. Yes Scotland's early plans used flimsy premises and weak empirical evidence, but precisely because of this, improvements could be drastic. If these flaws are corrected, we can reach potential untapped support, and win the referendum. In this chapter we explain the campaign's failings, and propose an alternative strategy.

Elements of the Yes Strategy

Nationalist thinkers believe they won in 2011 because they discovered a formula: continuity plus optimism equals victory. This political alchemy, they insist, works in any context, and the independence case is invincible so long as they never stray. So how would this abstract formula apply in practical terms?

For continuity, they present independence as a linear progression of devolution. Holyrood is, in relative terms, popular: while about a third of Scotland, for decades, has wanted to abolish Britain, only 6 per cent want Scotland's Parliament to be abolished.[4] Approval ratings for the Scottish Government and its policies lie at 53 per cent, compared to 25 per cent for Westminster.[5] And most Scots support devolution max, that is, Holyrood taking power over all issues except foreign policy, defence and immigration.[6]

To win, therefore, Yes Scotland presents independence as an evolution of devolution. The existing social order will stay intact, but a few administrative tasks will move to Edinburgh, and with the prospect of Tory rule in London, who would object? Salmond explains that Scotland belongs to six unions, five of which – currency, monarchy, society, Europe and defence – a Yes vote preserves.[7] Only the parliamentary union with Westminster will be disturbed, a vision that amounts to 'independence lite', as the first minister concedes.[8] As Gerry Hassan notes, it positions independence as 'an expression of traditional Scotland, as being about continuity and preservation, rather than fundamental change … a kind of "devolution max plus"'.

> One senior SNP politician once told us, 'All independence entails is extending the Scotland Act until it covers all Scottish domestic life.' They then sat back satisfied with the straightforwardness of it. 'It's that simple,' they concluded. Such an approach explicitly positions independence as a politics of gradualism and incremental change, and as the child of devolution.[9]

Better Together made their campaign strategy clear from the start, and it has never varied. They seek to create a climate of fear and emergency, appealing to conservative instincts by warning that the sky will fall after independence. Scotland's media, driven by sensationalism more than bias, are complicit in this tactic, forecasting 9/11-style terrorist attacks, currency meltdowns and even cruder disaster scenarios.[10]

Early on, Salmond's allies positioned independence in centrist terms to deter these assaults. Rather than confront scare stories with facts, they sought to soothe public fears by shifting ground. Thus, the SNP ended decades of opposition to NATO, the nuclear alliance that polices Russian influence in Europe, which demoralised supporters and lost them two MSPs. They also insisted, defying concerns from some Yes Scotland chiefs, that the pound sterling would stay Scotland's currency after independence. Republican ideas gain little attention, and the SNP insist that elected Scottish leaders will bow and scrape before Elizabeth's successors. So independence will free us from the unpopular, albeit elected, shadow of the House of Commons. But many of the most undemocratic features of British statehood will continue, to appease fear of change. These are the same undemocratic institutions – ancestral rule, militarism, Bank of England – that make Westminster democracy a farce.

Complementing this stress on continuity, the second part of strategy is unrelenting optimism. Leaders often repeat the scriptural lesson of 2011: the SNP won because it was positive, Labour lost because it was negative. This is now an unshakeable article of faith, a truism trumping all logic and empirical evidence. Yes campaign chief strategist Stephen Noon claims that 'one of the most powerful lessons' he has learned is that 'positive campaigning will beat negative campaigning.'[11] Alex Salmond is another believer in the formula's magical properties: 'When there are two negative campaigns, the most negative campaign usually wins. But when you have a positive campaign and a negative campaign, the positive will always win.'[12]

Yes officials explain that optimism must be relentless because any negative toxin will spoil the alchemy. 'A mixed message, sometimes up, sometimes down, does not work as well,' Noon argues.[13] He claims to base this conclusion on scientific research: analysis of twentieth-century US elections proves that positive campaigns always win and 'the more optimistic the campaign was, the bigger the eventual majority.'[14] Boosterism and hype thus replaces substance and policy as the root cause of success. Rather than contrast Britain today with what Scotland should achieve, we should contrast the 'optimism' of our campaign with the 'pessimism' of theirs.

Both parts of the Yes campaign's strategy – continuity and optimism – seem to reflect pragmatic concerns. We want victory, after all, and general assumptions about the causes of political success can help us win. Nevertheless, on these grounds, Noon's hegemony has not turned Yes Scotland into a vote-winning colossus. Perhaps, then, he presumes implicit, untested ideas that should be detailed and revised.

As we mentioned, Noon's acolytes remove policy from referendum strategy and reduce political communication to a dichotomy, positive and negative. But policy can never truly disappear: instead, positive messaging aims for indistinct promises that reassure everyone. Thus, Noon smuggles a conservative social blueprint – one-nation Scotland – under blanket optimism. By similar logic, Yes Scotland has been designed to appeal equally to all social classes in Scotland. So sociology disappears from strategy; but ignoring sociology involves inevitable sociological assumptions. Principally, it assumes that the formula 'handing back power to the Scottish people' will be vague enough to appeal to everyone. But different social groups need 'power' for different reasons. Empowerment means saving jobs, the NHS and free education, for working-class people; for elites, it means lower taxes and privatisation.

What could unite these divergent interests? Essentially, the Yes Scotland campaign has two options. One stresses Scotland's independent value system, comparing Scots' egalitarian spirit to South-east England's yuppie individualism that resigns us to Tory governments. Cases like the bedroom tax and £9,000 student fees show clear divergences between Westminster and Holyrood, and many believe these moral differences are the engine of a better society after 2014. Another method is to stress cross-class, unconditional advantages accruing from a Yes vote. Council house tenants and Morningside bankers both gain from scrapping Trident and better management of North Sea oil, say Yes officials.

Why It Won't Work

These points have merits, but they offer a slim platform to assess the gains of independence, hindering visions of real alternatives to the status quo. Few deny Scotland's different moral climate to parts of England. The Tory Party, whose membership reflects centuries of privileged, cosy relations between English capitalism and the landed classes, still dominates rural constituencies and the South East, but they are unelectable in Scotland. UKIP, an emerging force in English elections, is a joke north of the border. But while Scottish politics may have different aspirations in aggregate terms, this conceals great unevenness and dubious assumptions.[15] Indeed,

Holyrood politicians and Scottish councils imposed pro-market reforms with vigour equal to that of their English counterparts (see Chapter 3), despite an ostensible consensus for social democracy.

As for unconditional benefits, no one suffers from removing Trident missiles from the Clyde. While a small number of jobs are located at Faslane, they could be redeployed to productive civilian uses at far lower cost.[16] Estimated at £85 billion, a Trident replacement is extortionate, and the so-called 'security benefits' are outweighed by the risks. Even militarists and Conservative Scots question the value of these investments, and thus Yes Scotland can call for a nuclear-free Scotland with no costs.

They can also assume a degree of consensus on North Sea oil. While many dispute its long-term future, and worry about unstable oil prices, Scots are aware that Westminster squandered a huge opportunity to rebuild our economy. An independent treasury, no matter how incompetent, would make better use of Scotland's offshore resources. Thatcher, after all, snatched these revenues to bankroll her experiment in monetarist economics, ruining much of Scottish industry.[17] Thus, a discovery that should have re-energised Scotland helped consign communities to decades of misery. While a few Edinburgh financiers, and certain Grampian postcodes, became very wealthy, most of Scotland did not profit from North Sea oil.

But moving beyond Trident and oil, what promises about independence would benefit 'all of Scotland'? The Yes case has few details because no similar policies exist.

This poses problems for a positive strategy. With so few concrete promises, what precisely are we optimistic about? Optimism, as Barbara Ehrenreich points out, is not the same as hope, and with very little to promise, we are jollied into a 'hopeless optimism'.[18] With nothing specific to offer, we retreat into optimism about being Scottish, a bloodless civic identity politics.

Problems of economic and political structure become psychological malfunctions, as we are exposed to endless pleas to 'overcome the Scottish cringe'. Scots, according to nationalist intellectuals, are existentially displaced, and lack a sense of national purpose. Hence, they are gloomy and pessimistic, treating their traditions with contempt, labouring under an inferiority complex. Indeed, many extend this a step further, claiming, with self-help gurus like Carol Craig, that Scotland's spiritual diffidence causes its social problems.[19] Scots' egalitarianism, they argue, stifles initiative and degrades success. Better Together figures share similar ideas. 'We have been battling to shed what people called the Scottish cringe, which has suffocated individual ambitions, for generations,' argues Scottish Lib Dem leader Willie Rennie MSP. 'So we need to be careful that we do not, in our desire to remain in the UK, simply compound the problem by playing to the historical narrative.'[20] He admonishes his own supporters to 'talk up Scotland', and not to fall into the negativity trap.

The Yes campaign has absorbed these conformist assumptions about the 'national psyche'. So where Scots are not voting for independence, the cause is insufficient faith in Scottish identity. Hence, Noon and his acolytes believe that winning means making Scots share their optimism: optimism, that is, about being Scottish.

If anyone doubts this formula, SNP officials insist, look at Obama's 2008 victory, which redefined modern campaigning. But even on this definitive example, caveats emerge. True, Obama's memorable slogan 'Yes we can' is optimistic, but a closer inspection of the election elicits forgotten subtleties. He based his positive message on his (then) assured status as the Bush administration's most powerful critic on Iraq and Wall Street, and this 'negative' reputation allowed him to oust Hillary Clinton for the Democratic nomination. And throughout the election, Obama's team ran adverts defaming opponents' integrity, which is negative campaigning in the strong sense of *ad hominem* slurs.

Thus, the clichéd story of Obama's positive vibes does not resemble his campaign's reality. And by the assumptions of Stephen Noon, it should be doubly dubious, since he claims that only a *100 per cent positive* campaign can win; indeed, any remote hint of negativity or mixed messages will spoil the effect, and the most negative will win. Noon also insists that his formula extends well beyond Obama's, and claims to have proof that positive candidates always win. But Noon's research is shaky at best: the paper he cites as evidence analyses a sample of just one speech from each presidential candidate. Even the study's authors caution against generalising from such limited data.[21]

None of these reservations means we believe the opposite, that relentless negativity is a winning formula. Instead, we insist that reducing politics to a positive–negative dichotomy is indefensible in practical and intellectual terms. Noon et al. trade on a vicious double-meaning in the term 'negative', which can mean *ad hominem* insults and slanders – which no one wants, although many still rely on, including Obama – but it can also mean a strategy that takes a critical stance towards the failings of the status quo. Hence, a platitude – 'nobody likes a negative campaign', that is, personal attacks – is elevated as grounds for stasis and conservatism in policy terms. Building a platform on such shaky premises poses serious problems in practice.

But Yes Scotland's most glaring difficulties stem from the continuity part of the equation. By accepting that change equals danger, they have fallen into Better Together's trap, allowing unionists to set the framework for 'stability'. This creates very curious omissions. No doubt, many people want reassurance that their children will have better opportunities than they had. But do British institutions stabilise living standards?

On many fronts, the UK is the least stable nation state in Northern Europe. Britain's security may be measured, in the first case, by exposure to political violence. New Labour and the Tories both backed the Bush administration in the Middle East, they said, to deter future terror attacks. But in reality, it achieved the opposite: when Islamists use violence against Britain, from the Glasgow airport bombing to the murder of Lee Rigby, they cite the occupation of Iraq. Even establishment figures admit the 'War on Terror' made Britain a terrorist target.[22] 'The UK is at particular risk because it is the closest ally of the United States,' according to the Royal Institute of International Affairs.[23] Association with Britain's violence in the Middle East makes Scotland a potential target for reprisals.

The British economic model also destabilises living standards. For more than three decades, UK governments competed through deregulation, debt, low taxes and privatisation, and change on these fronts is improbable, leaving the UK vulnerable to repeats of the 2008 crisis. Indeed, things are getting worse, after Britain lost its AAA credit rating, and Con-Dem austerity sabotaged recovery rates. Thus, 'stability' has a loaded meaning. In the British sense, it means stabilising the fortunes of the very wealthy, while most people's livelihoods suffer.

Continuity with the UK model, in geopolitics, economics, or social affairs, means inevitable instability. But Scotland's media act as if the referendum is making life volatile. Yes Scotland is acclimatised to this unionist concept of stability, and thus presents change in moderate and incremental language.

Of course, voters want reassurances, but stability covers a variety of anxieties, from the fear of losing one's pension or bus pass, to the fear of having landholdings confiscated by an angry mob of crofters. Yes Scotland allows the No campaign to dictate the terms of debate, and scrabbles around responding on a piecemeal basis. This demoralises activists and confuses voters about the purpose and ambition of independence, while emboldening unionists in all parts of Scottish society.

Beyond Yes Scotland

These conservative voices do not dominate independence campaigning. While the official Yes headquarters neurotically stage-manages everything, the overall movement has spawned new forms of cooperation and political vision that look beyond tribal boundaries. The Common Weal, the Radical Independence Campaign and National Collective are three such examples. This shows the potential of the Yes campaign. The contrast with Better Together, which has virtually no links to extra-parliamentary politics, is stark. While we have serious intellectual disagreements with Yes leaders, we are committed to winning a Yes vote. Our strategy for victory highlights two missing components: the question of Britain and the question of class division in Scotland.

Yes campaigners accept a variety of views about the problems of UK capitalism, and there is room for disagreement. But convincing Scots to feel more Scottish is a definite losing strategy. Polling evidence shows that Scottish identity has weak correlation with voting patterns.[24] Our task in common, across the Yes movement, is convincing Scots that they lose out from attachments to Britain.

This task is complicated because attitudes to Britishness are contradictory. Many older Scots are nostalgic for the progressive gains of the post-war era, remembering a Britain that took the lead in defeating Nazism and building socialised housing and medicine. They still believe that Britain, under Labour, can improve their lives. Others are attached to the purely kitschy elements of its nationalism, from the glamour of Will and Kate to the spectacle of the Olympics. Beyond this, pockets of sympathy for British chauvinism persist. Although organised fascism in Scotland is weak, anti-Irish and anti-Asian bigotry persists.

But even those with the ugliest attachments to British identity are winnable to independence on radical grounds, because backward ideas coexist with progressive ideas. Those who back the UK because they are loyal to the Queen, for instance, may hate the bedroom tax or NHS privatisation. Trying to persuade them that independence is a better home for monarchist views is futile – Britain will always appeal to conservative instincts – but we can convince them that Scotland's resources could be managed in their interests. Those who have sentimental or tribal links to Labour are our most significant constituency. We must show them how Westminster has rendered reforms near impossible, and how Labour's attachment to American imperialism limits any initiative Britain-wide.

Political sociology should guide our strategy. Different classes in Scotland have different interests, and voting for independence is not a wise move for Scottish elites. They already have the most pro-business regime in Europe under Westminster, no matter which party wins elections. Why would they vote for an uncertain alternative? Nobody should be surprised when polls show that nine out of ten businesses favour a No vote. Attempting to stay neutral and speak for Scotland as a whole is misguided. By failing to defend working-class needs, and focusing messages on opinion-formers, they assume that 'ordinary' people possess no independent initiative. Tellingly, at the first STUC consultation on independence in Glasgow, Yes Scotland sent a former Tory candidate and 'entrepreneur' to convince trade unionists. Labour, knowing their audience, sent a former shop steward. The cause of these embarrassments is a characteristic blindness to social class.

This is despite clear and long-established evidence of sociological divides on constitutional questions. In the 1979 referendum, a majority of working-class Scots voted for an Assembly (57 per cent), which most middle-class voters (60 per cent) opposed.[25] Even in 1997, where home rule was backed by all classes, support was far higher among working (91 per cent) than middle-class Scots (69 per cent). Scotland's plumbers and cleaners dragged reluctant shop owners, GPs, and academics with them. Winning workers was necessary before winning professionals and managers; and big business, on aggregate, will always concede change last.

Today, the numbers are clear. MORI polling shows support for independence is highest in deprived (58 per cent) rather than affluent areas (27 per cent).[26] Earlier polls by TMS-BRMB showed the same, consistent higher support among working-class Scots. Building on this support is not enough; reaching these groups before the referendum must be a priority. The most likely Yes voters are the least likely to register to vote, and this should guide an effective approach to 'grass-roots campaigning', built on the geography of Scotland's social classes. The actual Obama campaign, as opposed to its later mythology, won because it understood where real people live, and registered them to vote. Spreading a windy aura of change, without defining who will gain, leads to weak thinking. Independence will be won in tower blocks, housing estates and small towns, not gated communities or rural mansions.

Of course, alone, reaching out to people is not enough. To win a Yes vote, we need a message that balances a vision of social change with a critique of present society. Trust in politicians has never been lower, and this makes people wary of alternatives, but, ironically, Better Together capitalise on pessimism about UK democracy. This suggests where the Yes campaign's intrinsic advantages lie, in the critique of Westminster, and why hopeless optimism will fail. As James Maxwell observes in the *New Statesman*:

> A more effective Yes campaign would balance its aspirational account … with a critique of the British state, highlighting the democratic and international costs Scotland pays for remaining part of the UK. In particular, it would make clear the link between Scotland's abysmal social record (one of the worst in western Europe) and the concentration of political and economic power in London and the south east. It would also aim to systematically undermine the Scottish public's confidence in …Westminster … even if this means abandoning its much vaunted commitment to positive campaigning. The one thing it can't afford to do is spend [time] responding to aggressive unionist and media questioning.[27]

Better Together will continue to question Scotland's stability. Can we afford to go it alone? Can we withstand another crisis? Rather than shift to make room for these crafty issues, the Yes camp should turn the questions back on Britain and the British state. Can we afford to stay in Britain? Can present trends continue? How committed is Westminster to reining in the financial sector? If the City of London continues to dictate our economic policy, how long will we last until the next economic crisis, and who will pay for it?

The referendum can be won, but only if independence campaigners set the agenda, rather than deflecting attacks from Better Together. Our starting-point should be the failure of the present settlement in Britain. Most people are already convinced, at some level, that in terms of fairness, democracy and the environment, the way we do things in Britain is unsustainable. Something needs to change. If we miss this link, and accept the equation of continuity with stability, Better Together has won already. By assuming people want more of the same, we make sure they will act accordingly, by voting No.

If we want to avoid this, we need to build an appetite for change. This means stressing the need for a social alternative that puts the needs of Scotland's people above corporate profits. Societies around the world do better than Britain, and hence putting our resources to better use is not beyond us. These statements might alienate Yes Scotland's business supporters, but their potential to sway disenchanted Labour voters is massive. The trade unions, despite their links to Labour, can bridge the economic and political divide in democracy, if their membership is activated. In the next chapter, we outline in more detail what institutions and policies we should establish.

Changing the campaign can reinvigorate our support. In 1995, Quebec held its own independence referendum, and in the year approaching it, opinion polls consistently showed two-thirds opposition. But with only three weeks to go, the leader of the Yes campaign was replaced and the campaign changed direction, prompting a massive swing towards the Yes vote. By polling day, they were level; in the end, they lost by less than 1 per cent. There are no guarantees that this will happen in Scotland. But it shows how quickly things can change, and the difference an effective campaign can make. Despite the many setbacks the Yes campaign has suffered since its launch, we are not pessimistic.

6

Scotland vs the Twenty-first Century: Towards a Radical Needs Agenda

Britain's direction under Thatcher and Blair disenchanted millions and froze the working class out of politics, but how exceptional was the UK in this respect? Was New Labour not just complying with standard neoliberal practice, dictated by transnational corporations and financiers? To varying degrees, the horrors of UK capitalism recur in every economy, and for several decades all nation states have been sucked into a 'race to the bottom'. Governments elbowed others aside to offer corporations tax breaks, subsidies, legal immunity, cheap labour, and various kickbacks. The mobility of investment and property has aided this, spreading political and economic insecurity across the globe, as states sacrifice welfare programmes on the altar of competition. In this sense, Britain emerges not as a deviant case, but as conforming to external agendas beyond its control. If so, should we not question the game itself, as opposed to the player?

Persuasive as this appears, it conceals the characteristics of British capitalism. No doubt, most capitalist states privatised resources and lowered taxes on the rich, but Britain's rates were astonishing for a democratic society. This was not just a normal state complying with the rules: the UK set new rules. Having been one of the most equal advanced economies, in a few decades, it has become one of the most divided.

Moreover, as we have shown in Chapter 1, Britain's big businesses and its military forces are indivisible; and their imperial alliance with the US helps secure global inequalities. While many nations surrendered to the global market, others required coercion. Where countries deviated from 'Washington Consensus' economics, they were punished, either by coups and destabilisation, or by invasion. Britain did not join every Pentagon aggression or CIA coup, but the UK's security services were never far away, and the UK offers diplomatic cover in the United Nations for the US and allies such as Israel. In this sense, Britain goes beyond following neoliberal norms: it enforces them.

Britain might have regained its place in the top rank of global nations, in a sense, by ransacking its public services and cheerleading market forces. But Britain's working class made the sacrifices for this new 'global purpose'. As Richard Wilkinson and Kate Pickett remark:

> If Britain became as equal as [Japan, Norway, Sweden and Finland], levels of trust might be expected to be two-thirds as high again as they are now, mental illness might be more than halved, everyone would get an additional year of life, teenage birth rates could fall to one-third of what they are now, homicide rates could fall by 75 per cent, everyone could get the equivalent of almost seven weeks extra holiday a year, and the government could be closing prisons all over the country.[1]

Critics note many problems with the Nordic and Japanese varieties of capitalism, but to say they are preferable is not to have illusions about them. Elsewhere, we may observe, states deviate from the US-UK model without falling apart. Quite the opposite: many of these economies are more competitive than the UK's, as well as healthier and happier. Indeed, the greater the divergence, the better the performance, in terms of social indicators.

In an era of global regression, trends in the UK reflect those across the world in exaggerated form, so views on the UK model diverge on left–right affiliations of ideology. For those who see citizens as costs to be lowered at every opportunity, Britain is a utopia. In this perfect order, democratic oversight is cursory, workers' rights are minimised by punitive legislation, and the state is reduced to its authoritarian core. Within a few decades, every society will resemble the UK, that harbinger of progress, if we believe neoliberals.

For those who put social justice before private profit, the UK model stands for everything that makes the present social order unsustainable. Hence, a true internationalist does not seek to protect the British state. A true internationalist strives for an alternative, and wishes to prove that the British model is not inevitable, to weaken the global drift into minimal market democracy. For radicals, alternatives are workable as well as necessary, and the task is to break societies from neoliberal conformity.

Of course, Scottish independence involves far more than radical politics, and the Yes movement allows for many visions of a future Scotland, some of them sinister. Michael Russell and like-minded nationalists prefer a low-tax Caledonian free-for-all, competing with South Asia, the Baltic countries and Southern Europe. Others aspire to a Nordic utopia with regulated banking and strong welfare provision (see Chapter 4). Reducing the essence of Scottish independence to either blueprint is foolish, although many are determined to do so. Left-wing unionists sometimes insist that Scottish independence is a conspiracy designed to give Brian Souter his neoliberal wonderland. But limiting Scottish sovereignty to one man's wet dream is as nonsensical as reducing Britain's destiny to the epic fantasies of bow-tie-wearing Tories named Torquil who want a flat tax, a quick EU exit, and to restore Britain's glory by re-conquering the Sudan. Even if Scottish voters crowned Brian Souter monarch after independence, his agenda would meet ferocious resistance. The case, as we explained in earlier chapters, applies the other way. Even if we could come up with a Nordic plan, and win an election on this basis, we would meet built-up opposition from across Scottish society.

Alternative visions of Scotland still have a valuable role in the 2014 debate. Perhaps the Left has been too reluctant to do this, seeing utopias as illusions, and 'sober class analysis' as the key to changing society. But we live in an age of 'capitalist realism', as Mark Fisher calls it, with 'the widespread sense that not only is capitalism the only viable political and economic system, but also that it is now impossible even to *imagine* a coherent alternative to it.'[2] In this environment, any radical vision can be subversive. But we should not get drunk on utopias either, so instead of outlining a blueprint for socialism per se, which depends on international conditions, our proposals are more modest. We call it a 'revolution of radical needs', after Marx.[3] In this chapter, we outline what putting the interests of Scotland's people before private capital would involve.

Social Justice

'By building a more dynamic and faster growing economy we will increase prosperity, be better placed to tackle Scotland's health and social challenges, and establish a fairer and more equal society,' says the Scottish Government.[4] Every Holyrood government presents the same formula, balancing social justice with economic growth, but very few specify its meaning. What is a 'fair' distribution of resources in society? And is it possible to square the market model of economic growth with any notion of fairness or justice?

In its most minimal sense, social justice has been defined as equality of opportunity, a scenario where accidents of birth do not decide social outcomes. In this model of a just society, children of aristocrats have the same chance of working in Tesco as the children of plumbers or call-centre workers. Big differences of salary would persist, to foster 'talent' and 'enterprise'; but every baby would have an equal prospect of reaching the top, or the bottom, of the ladder.

Many criticise the limits of this definition, and we sympathise with the critiques. Social justice, in our view, ought to involve equality of outcome, and we favour a cooperative economy over market competition. But the minimal definition allows us to examine the aspirations of social democracy today. Are governments making sure every citizen gets a fair chance, that accidents of birth no longer influence outcomes? Are states protecting people from other accidents beyond their control, such as illness, unemployment, and old age?

Even this minimal concept of fairness and equality has endured sustained attack for decades, and the prospect of equalising incomes has vanished. Indeed, the trend has been *regressive* – the rich are getting richer at the expense of the poor – with the UK leading the curve. Polly Toynbee, among others, attributes this to public apathy: 'Post-Thatcher, fewer people seem to question why incomes are distributed as they are. Conservative cultural domination of a generation has atrophied natural sensitivity to the unfairness of the accidents of birth or position.'[5]

But mounting evidence suggests that a large part of the population does care. Since the Thatcher era, over 80 per cent of Britain has held the view that the gap in incomes between rich and poor is too large.[6] This number peaked in 1995 (87 per cent). Attitudes to wealth, as opposed to income, are somewhat softer, but the numbers who think that 'ordinary working people' do not get their fair share have rarely dropped below 60 per cent. Do these common sentiments add to a mood for government action? Here, the numbers are vaguer, but the statistics show a good section of the population in Scotland (43 per cent) and even England (34 per cent) favour state action to move wealth from rich to poor.[7]

Would voters sacrifice growth for justice? This depends on perceptions of the scale of the crisis. At various times in history, it has been necessary to put normality on hold. During both World Wars, for instance, the ordinary working of markets was suspended, the economy was centralised and planned, and rationing was introduced in place of the market. Even Britain and the US operated a sort of 'War Communism': to gain society-wide cooperation, the wartime burden had to be shared. The result was full employment and a narrowing in income differences, and life expectancy increased by record numbers, despite bombs falling overhead.

And today, when a bank is too big to fail, governments are quite happy to drop the taboo of nationalisation. Here, of course, the 'shared burden' falls on taxpayers, who pay the price for risks taken by bankers. Likewise, even the most extreme free market fanatics will move to protect national industries when they come under threat from competition. George W. Bush's populist protection of the American steel industry is a clear example of this.

What links these examples is the concept of 'emergency', where the urgency of a particular situation forces the suspension of the private market. Sadly, the needs of society's rulers, rather than those who suffer from their decisions, define what counts as an emergency. So what would qualify as a true emergency?

In our view, the present gulf in incomes must be defined in these terms. The coincidence of obscene wealth and dire poverty is stark. The richest 1,000 saw their wealth bulge from £99 billion to £301 billion in the nine years of Blair in power,[8] and the top 10 per cent (or the top 100) increased their share from 47 to 54 per cent in a similar period.[9] This is the universe of *Made in Chelsea* and Pippa Middleton, as well as Mohammed Al-Fayed, Roman Abramovich and the Glazer family. In 2010, CEO pay in the UK increased by 49 per cent, and, according to a report by the European Banking Authority, 2,500 UK bankers earned over €1 million per year, compared to 162 in France and 36 in the Netherlands.[10] Even in Scotland, the wealthiest households are 273 times richer than the poorest, Oxfam have noted.[11] The number of £1 million homes spiked 14 per cent in Scotland in the recession year of 2012, compared to a figure for the rest of the UK of 2 per cent.

In a famous incident, Blair claimed to have no concerns that those earning £34,000 per year and those on £34 million pay the same tax rates. 'It's not a burning ambition for me to make sure that David Beckham earns less money,' he retorted. But many British tycoons pay little tax at all. Tax fraud costs UK taxpayers £70 billion annually, compared to the £1 billion cost of benefit fraud.[12] But do tax-evading elites receive seventy times more media slander than 'benefit cheating chavs'?

Research shows poverty in Scotland is worse than it has been for 30 years. As of 2013, 14 per cent of Scots – 720,000 people – live in a state of basic deprivation, according to official statistics.[13] Forty per cent of those in poverty are in work, and this is likely to increase, since the number forced into part-time work against their will doubled from 2008–12.[14] One hundred thousand Glaswegians use payday loans to meet everyday expenses. Between 2011–12 and 2012–13, the Citizens' Advice Bureau noted a *threefold* increase in contact from people in Glasgow in desperate debt circumstances. The bedroom tax scandal has highlighted the risk of destitution and homelessness in Scottish communities.

A recent report by the Centre for Analysis of Social Exclusion at the LSE suggests Britain will have Victorian-level inequality by 2025 if we continue on the current path.[15] In earlier decades, normality has been suspended because 'Islamic terrorism' poses a threat to the 'fundamental values of our civilisation'. This tells us a lot about what our elites consider 'basic' to our society. By continuing to conform to the British model, we will suffer a far greater emergency of poverty and declining opportunity. Something has to change, and quickly.

Environmental Justice

An equal, perhaps greater, emergency is climate change. The dangers here are not confined to any one society; they are about the prospects of a liveable planet for future generations. Unless governments act to minimise the damage of carbon emissions and pollution, the prognosis is bleak. Indeed, many respected scientists believe our economy has driven the earth beyond possible recovery, although this is disputed. All sides agree, however, that drastic changes are needed; the question is how the burden will be shared. This poses a stark question. Can we reconcile the market mode of economic growth with the basics of environmental justice?

If we continue with the US-UK model, this will prove impossible (see Figures 6.1 and 6.2). At best, we can hope for a succession of miraculous technological breakthroughs, but even then, the UK spends a very small part of its R&D budget on climate change, since other ventures, like pharmaceutical patents and weapons, are far more profitable. Estimates suggest we need to cut carbon emissions by 87 per cent by 2030.[16] Ernst and Young forecast the UK needs to spend £450 billion between 2010 and 2025 just to meet our current climate targets, but existing sources of

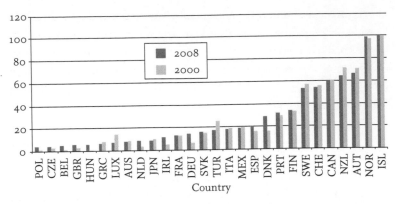

Figure 6.1   Share of renewables in electricity production

Source: B. Boitier, 'CO$_2$ emissions production-based accounting vs consumption: Insights from the WIOD databases' and OECD

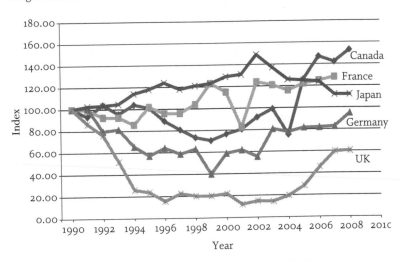

Figure 6.2   Index of government 'Green' energy R&D budgets

Source: OECD Economic Surveys: United Kingdom – © OECD 2011

funding will give just £50–80 billion.[17] A profound change in social order is necessary to fill this £400 billion black hole without massive injustice. But at present, the UK, along with the US and Australia, still leads the way in subsiding its *fossil fuel* industry.[18] Britain maintains a carbon-based political order, and change is slow, when it should, and must, be drastic.

Are pro-market thinkers ignoring the emergency of climate? Things are not that simple, since corporations are speculating about potential profits from green investment and think-tank gurus propose using the market to make pollution unprofitable. Consumers, they assert, will become educated about their decisions, and will boycott companies that pollute, and will buy green products instead. If necessary, the government should introduce incentives to private business, such as tax cuts for green start-ups. Others are in favour of a system of carbon trading, a capitalistic approach to carbon rationing. This market already amounts to $64 billion, according to World Bank figures.

These solutions are flawed on two counts. First, market approaches downplay the scale of the climate emergency. If recent economic trends continue, large parts of the planet will be uninhabitable for humans as well as for millions of other species. The cost of melting Arctic sea ice alone could be $60 trillion, nearing global GDP, if the thawing permafrost triggers the release of methane from the East Siberian Sea.[19] Poor and developing countries will suffer most of these costs, according to scientific and economic research. This presents just one of many looming catastrophes, and the present scale of action is insufficient.

Secondly, the market solution is flawed in sharing equal blame between poor people and powerful economic actors. The richest 1 per cent of US society, for instance, use *10,000 times* more carbon than the average American; they can afford to live with far less.[20] The same logic applies to rich and poor countries. Neoliberals expect developing economies to endure equal cuts to the likes of the US, even though these nations bear the costs (estimated at $1.2 trillion per year) of carbon emissions resulting from decisions in the West. Barring fundamental change, these grim trends can continue without limits of justice, safety, or precedent. Doing nothing but 'managing' the present settlement would thus normalise a profound environmental injustice.

If we continue on the present path, the path of Britain and the US, we will find ourselves on the wrong side of the moral and social cleavages of the twenty-first century. Whether societies can fuse 'growth' with social and environmental justice is an open question. But *market-led* growth will exacerbate the trends of the past forty years. That means the rich get richer, and their children get their jobs, the effect of climate change will spiral beyond our control, and rich elites will pursue resource competition by violent means. The costs of all this will be felt at the bottom, in teeming global slums in the South and marginalised housing estates in the North. None of this may be reconciled with fulfilling the elementary principles of justice.

So the twenty-first century poses a stark question: do we continue with the current path of private ownership and market anarchy, accepting that present trends will continue? Or do we socialise property under democratic control? Scotland's referendum is on the cusp of this problem. Britain, after all, is the paragon of neoliberal excellence, the star pupil of global elites, having followed every commandment in the market rulebook. Only Australia and the US rival the UK for a cross-party commitment to the authoritarian market model.

This trajectory, we suggest, is sustainably unsustainable. In formal terms, it can rumble on in crisis management mode; but if it becomes a general model, it will make the planet and human society unliveable. Real choices between markets and planning do not exist. Only sustainable and unsustainable futures exist; the pathological trends of the present, and the alternatives. Conformity is not an option: a better order must emerge for the sake of human survival. As Naomi Klein has said, '[D]itching [this] cruel system in favour of something new ... [is] no longer a matter of mere ideological preference but rather one of species-wide existential necessity.'[21]

Radical Democracy

The tasks of Labour-style social democracy used to be seen as the progressive achievement of civil, political and social rights.[22] After a fashion, our rights would advance so far that we would achieve a fair society. But today, all of these gains are being stolen, and the last four decades prove that social progress can roll backwards as well as leap forwards. Just as poverty and inequality are hitting 'Victorian' levels, so we are returning to a Victorian idea of minimal democracy in Britain's Bullingdon era.

Scotland endured the worst effects of Thatcher despite not voting Tory. Many called this the 'democratic deficit', an apt term, but Scotland's relation with Iron Maggie is just a metaphor for a far broader predicament. All societies are undergoing a democratic recession. As we would expect, Britain is at the vanguard of this trend; already lacking a constitution and labouring under the first-past-the-post system, what remains of citizen power has been eroded by the neoliberal era. Independence would be pointless if it meant more of this, and reversing the democratic deficit, in the widest possible sense, should be one of our central aims. But are there alternatives? Or is scepticism and 'apathy' about democracy unavoidable?

Not all societies suffered the same democratic losses. Outside the West, nations overturned dictatorships and received elections as liberations, and their later experiments did not always repeat the worst elements of neoliberalism. In small pockets of the world, there have been dramatic and successful democratic alternatives that combine popular participation and redistribution of wealth and power.

For instance, Porto Alegre in Brazil has run a powerful experiment in participatory budgeting. Since the late 1980s, under the rule of the left-of-centre Workers Party (PT), spending decisions in the city have been made by neighbourhood assemblies. Thousands of citizens, rich and poor, take part in two dozen annual assemblies, where residents debate and vote for funding priorities, and choose representatives who meet weekly to carry out the wishes of the community. They could resolve, for instance, whether to prioritise fixing a road, building a bridge, or setting up a cooperative day care centre.

Citizens are thus empowered to make decisions, and to administer the distribution of resources at a local level. The focus is on finding pragmatic solutions to local problems that matter in a neighbourhood, college, or workplace. The result, overall, has been drastic increases in popular participation, reduced corruption and inequality, and political education for the lowest socio-economic communities. Efforts to extend the model have been uneven, but each project has scored successes. Similar experiments have been carried out in Venezuela, Ecuador and India.

Can it work in developed countries? First, let us not forget that Brazil has overtaken Britain in the league table of global economies. Secondly, although elements might seem very context specific, it presents a general principle, which sociologist Erik Olin Wright calls 'empowered participatory governance' (EPG). Despite what many think, Porto Allegre is not an example of anarchist-style direct democracy. It envisions a key role for planning and central coordination. As Wright notes:

> ... the institutional design involves linkages of accountability and communication that connect local units to muscular central power. These central offices – for instance the mayor's office or the headquarters of a police department or school system – can reinforce the quality of local democratic deliberation and problem-solving in a variety of ways: by coordinating and distributing resources; by solving problems that local units cannot address by themselves; by rectifying pathological or incompetent decision-making in failing groups; and by diffusing innovations and learning across boundaries.[23]

Moreover, the practice of EPG is linked to strategies by social movements to change the nature of the central (nation) state itself. They try to expand the influence of consumers of government services beyond the local level into a participatory framework of national coordination. This element of *strategy* is crucial. Even the most enthusiastic proponents of Porto Alegre will admit that it presents only a first step, not the end of the process. Using grassroots activism to transform the nation state is a perquisite for effective emancipation.

In our view, this offers a much better framework for devolving power than we have currently. Neil Davidson and colleagues present UK devolution as a neoliberal strategy designed to weaken democratic forces.[24] Devolving power can create a race to the bottom, with more agents competing against each other. This does not apply in a uniform pattern, of course, since the Scottish Parliament has often shielded Scots against the ugliest New Labour and Con-Dem policies. But Holyrood has not solved the democracy gap, or led to new models of participation, and it has presided over rising inequality.

A recent report by the Jimmy Reid Foundation testifies to these problems.[25] Seventy per cent of in-work people in Scotland earn less than £24,000 per year. But this group form just 3 per cent of those giving evidence to Holyrood committees, and 11 per cent of Scots on public bodies. Those who earn over £34,000 are a fraction of overall Scotland (13 per cent), but they form 70 per cent of those who influence policy. The present system excludes the vast majority from practical involvement in politics.

A proper model of radical democracy in Scotland would have to improve on Porto Alegre. Involving service consumers is not enough; weak democracy must be confronted at the level of economic ownership and control. The STUC represents 600,000 workers in Scotland, making it by far the largest democratic organisation in society. But its potential is virtual at present. Applying the general principles of EPG to workplaces is the next logical step to democratising society.

Beyond designing better models of local administration, we also need to find ways to curb the corporate control over elections and parliamentary politics. This means an alternative to the financial arrangements we have at present, which make democracy inaccessible to all but the biggest parties. Small parties cannot compete with millions of pounds from big business; and the model of trade union donations has legitimised the corruption of Labour Party governments, rather than keeping them under popular mandate.

One alternative, devised by American academic Bruce Ackerman and championed by Wright, is to give each citizen a $50 credit card that may only be used to finance election candidates.[26] Any nominee receiving funds from this source would be *banned* from taking other money. This would offer a cost-effective way of narrowing the gap between democracy and everyday life. Of course, the best-funded parties may opt to continue with corporate donations and cash-for-peerages, but it would at least make alternatives workable. If grass-roots funding was high enough, it could destroy the back-scratching donation system for good.

None of these solutions is enough to form an alternative to the neoliberal state, and the anti-democratic power of capitalism cannot be removed by a few reforms. But imagining these alternatives is a crucial, and sadly forgotten, part of the 2014 debate. To achieve the true social ownership and coordination of economic goods, we need a framework of radical democracy, of direct involvement of the population in administration. This would have to mix the principle of majority decision making and central coordination with decentralised governance.

Radical Economy

The capitalist model of growth is inconsistent with the needs of humanity and the challenges of the green economy. The more a nation conforms to the market model, the further it moves from any ability to tackle these issues. As far as possible, we need to overcome every feature of capitalist society, but this must be done at a global level. In the meantime, an anti-capitalist agenda means putting human equality and sustainability at the heart of economic policy. This will involve combining the efficiencies of planning and coordination with the democratic benefits of community participation. In other words, it means generalising Porto Alegre to economic decisions as a whole, moving beyond consumption to the hidden abode of production.

At present, we are only beginning to understand the elements of this. In a world economy dominated by profit and competition, are there any economic alternatives? Or will markets always force out any competing economic organisms?

In reality, great unevenness persists. Not every capitalist economy is as privatised as Britain, and we could take measures to reverse private control and increase the possibility of planning our resources. Planning for need is the only choice that supports a modicum of human and environmental security. So what components contribute to a radical agenda?

The obvious starting-point is nationalisation, despite its gloomy reputation in Britain. Until 2008, nationalised industries were seen as bywords for inefficiency; this reflected the success of Thatcherite ideology, since in reality their productivity kept pace with and often outmatched the private sector in the post-war era. For radical agendas, the major problems derived from two sources. First, nationalisation came at the behest of failing private owners, and management of these firms remained with traditional elites. Ownership was public, but decision making was not socialised. Keynesians, who dominated British economic thinking, were far more concerned with macro-economic targets than with how firms were run. Secondly, parliaments used profits from public resources to plug gaps elsewhere in the economy, rather than to re-invest in services. Thus, the UK endured long-term problems of under-investment.

But nationalisation is back. After all, this was the solution to the 'financial emergency' of Northern Rock, RBS and HBOS in 2007–08. Here, though, nationalisation was regressive in its impact, transferring wealth from poor to rich, to a massive degree. Nationalisation is a powerful weapon; the question is who wields it.

Leaving our core industries in private hands will prove a very dangerous move. If we want to move towards a green economy, we need control over two things, land and infrastructure, but at present, both of these are held by transnational or local elites. In the case of infrastructure, the companies that dominate this sector are legacies of privatisation, and many are controlled by external owners, who compete with each other, rather than planning to meet the needs of Scottish people. But this so-called 'market efficiency' did not, as was claimed, result in consumer sovereignty and reduced bills. In electricity and gas, prices are skyrocketing, and this hits the poorest hardest. For those in debt, costly pre-payment meters increase prices by £120 a year.[27] The richest, who consume the most heat and electricity, benefit from discounts for high-level consumers.

Caroline Lucas MP of the Green Party of England and Wales has led calls for a 'green new deal'.[28] This would involve £50 billion government spending on green technology over five years, including building green council housing to stop another round of booming house-price inflation. A 'carbon army' would be trained to insulate homes, which would slash fuel and energy costs for the poorest in society.

Will Scotland's existing energy interests cooperate with this agenda? Of course, the government may offer incentives and tax breaks in the low-carbon economy. But this piecemeal, incremental planning is far too limited. Scotland needs a holistic approach to green energy, which means using the profits from our infrastructure to rebalance the economy as a whole. The case of insulation highlights the radical inefficiencies of the private model. Private energy companies have no incentive to insulate poor peoples' homes, because their sole motive is profit, and the more energy consumed, the more their profits rise. Public companies could set the aim of reducing carbon emissions and prices for consumers, a far preferable scenario to the chaotic system of market allocation.

The case of land ownership is just as stark, with significant sections opposed to any change. *Half* of Scotland is under the control of 432 individuals, putting us among the most unequal countries in the developed world for land concentration. Until 2004, Scotland was, as Andy Wightman has argued, Europe's last feudal country.[29] Our lairds avoid an estimated £40 million in tax every year; meanwhile, in the most recent survey conducted, four of them were receiving lavish taxpayer subsidies of £1 million each, and many more were earning hundreds of thousands.

Among this number is the Duke of Buccleuch, a title created for the bastard son of Charles II in 1663; the duke is Europe's largest landowner with holdings valued at more than £1 billion.[30] But he is arguably not even the biggest land baron in the country. Many regard Danish tycoon Anders Holch Povlsen as the most powerful man in rural Scotland: he uses his property to rake in farming subsidies and avoid inheritance tax on his £4 billion fortune.[31] Scotland's land barons, Ian Davidson MP suggests, are the greediest benefit claimants in Britain.[32] These 'feudal' remnants have not survived by accident. They have a definite interest in preserving the status quo, and would resist, by force if necessary, democratic ownership of Scotland's natural resources.

Almost every economic plan for Scotland devises a role for green energy. But how can we achieve this, with such concentrated ownership? Even if the landlords can be convinced to support an anti-carbon agenda, if the *rents* of rural windfarms only profit this class, two things will happen. First, residents will oppose them. 'The public acceptance of windfarms in Denmark is largely due to the fact that most of them are owned by communities or co-operatives,' notes George Monbiot. 'The contrast to the UK could scarcely be greater, where communities fight tooth and nail against them, and planning objections are the major reason why the UK is struggling to meet its renewables targets.'[33] Britain has 4,000 wind turbines; Denmark has 6,000, despite being one-sixth the size of Britain, which may be because 70–80 per cent of Danish turbines are community owned.[34] Secondly, the Green New Deal in Scotland will have a shallow social base. The opportunity to use these necessary *ecological changes* to apply necessary *social change* will be lost.

Nationalisation is the best, but not the only, alternative to the market. Scotland at present has a cooperative economy worth £4.2 billion, and more should be done to protect this sector and give incentives to these enterprises. Worker-owned and community-owned cooperatives are often efficient, and many successful examples have broken the neoliberal mould. The Mondragon federation of worker cooperatives is the biggest company in the Basque region of Spain, employing 92,000. It has a turnover of €33 billion and is one of the largest manufacturing and financial firms in Spain.[35] The gap between executive pay and the lowest worker pay is set between 3:1 and 9:1, and at an average of 5:1. Italy has 10,000 producer-cooperatives, constituting vibrant parts of local economies. To achieve this, an independent Scotland should move beyond the community right-to-buy scheme. We should enshrine the right to own and manage companies as part of basic workers' rights. This would mean that workers or communities could vote to take over firms from management, and would be given cheap financing to allow this.

The market-based financial system is a major impediment to economic change. Of course, financial companies make big profits, and have been growing for decades, most of all in US-UK-style economies. But are they an efficient way of financing 'innovation'? The clear answer is no. Financial firms are not interested in overall economic efficiency; they aim to make profits for themselves. They have no obligations to the wider economy, and tend to harm it, by funnelling money into speculative investment in economic bubbles, and by using credit deregulation to push debt onto the poorest sectors of society. These activities have grown beyond reasonable limits in recent decades. Spending on research and development and productivity has fallen. The more finance relies on markets, the more it preferences short-term returns over stability. So, for these reasons, the US-UK societies are quite poor in innovation terms. Those innovations that they do make often have anti-social implications, for example, weapons and pharmaceutical patents.

Finally, a radical economic agenda must prioritise workers' rights. Britain has among the most draconian anti-union laws in Europe, making it illegal to show solidarity with fellow workers. By contrast, capitalist property experiences no hindrances in its right to strike, as was shown by the industrial dispute at Grangemouth in October 2013.[36] Attacks on union freedom undermine democracy and weaken the most vulnerable in society, and they should be reversed under independence.

Worst-Case Scenario

If the societies of the future are capitalist, this will present serious barriers to human development. But getting from here to an alternative society presents new problems. Since the 1970s, there has been a climate of fear around radical economic policies. Politicians, academics and the media are committed to the cult of capitalist realism, which suggests that the best route out of poverty is to let wealth 'trickle down' from the top. Any meddling in this, they suggest, will wreak havoc with the economy. Also, where countries have tried to wriggle free from capitalism, they have been isolated and attacked by the stronger nations in the world (that is, the US). If Scotland pursued a radical agenda, how would we deal with this?

First, the reality of any actually existing economy is far more nuanced. The market is one of many possible systems of economic cooperation, and even under capitalism, many parts of everyday life escape commodification. In every state today, the public sector still manages a huge part of economies. Without it, basic human needs and also basic market needs, such as cheap educated labour, would go unmet. A large part of investment finance is also socialised, in the form of pension and insurance funds. Although these are managed on market lines, and against the needs of the working people they serve, they are potential levers to socialise the economy. Retirement funds alone account for a quarter of UK public securities.[37] Finally, as we noted earlier, cooperatives have shown they can survive the harsh climate of globalisation. While markets will continue to retain coercive power, we should not fear exploring alternatives.

Better Together and the media promote scare stories in which Scotland becomes isolated from the 'world economy' and all the clever and rich people flee the country. What if Scotland's elites and investors went on strike? Of course, we might question the actual source of wealth: if every worker decided to withdraw their labour, there would be no profits to divvy up among managers, owners and financiers. Another angle is to look at the empirical record of countries who have tried to gain independence, either from colonialism, from a multi-national bloc, or from IMF/World Bank domination. Do countries that submit to neoliberalism fare better than countries pursuing radical policies?

In fact, the more a country concedes to international investors, we find, the worse its overall performance. Thus, Russia under Washington-engineered 'shock therapy' post-1991 suffered the largest peace-time economic collapse ever registered. Liberalisation, forced by impetuous global reformers, prefigured the East Asian crisis of 1997. The case of the Irish, Greek, Portuguese, Spanish and Italian economies is once again a sorry tale of privatisation, deregulation and ceding control of economic policy. Even in so-called 'neoliberal success stories', such as Pinochet's Chile and post-NAFTA Mexico, market experiments produced low wages and collapsing social services. Inequalities hit record highs, and living standards collapsed at the bottom.

By contrast, those countries that escape imperialist domination have fared better, or, at least, they performed well until being overthrown by the CIA. Even in cases where Washington has conspired with local elites to isolate radical nationalist and leftist regimes, the effect was never economic collapse. In the most extreme examples, the US uses its muscle to withdraw financing and resources, and to flood the society with propaganda supporting rich rulers. Where this failed, the CIA and native envoys would resort to a variety of violent tactics, from sabotage to mercenary death squads to assassination and coup attempts. The sorry history of Latin America, Asia and Africa in recent decades is testament to this.

But where radical governments have survived, they have been able to use their resources to better effect, despite the pressures of the world market. The longest lasting case was Cuba under Castro. Of course, Cuba's undesirable elements, from the militarisation of society to the lack of democracy at the top, are well documented. But what interests us here is the hostile environment it confronted. Cuba faced the two elements of a 'worst-case scenario'. First, the middle classes fled the country with their property, ideas and investments. Secondly, the United States tried to invade the country, and then imposed an illegal blockade, leaving Cuba isolated from global trade.

Did Cuba collapse? On the contrary, as the *Guardian* conceded:

Along with South Korea, Cuba probably has one of the most impressive and distinctive stories to tell in the annals of modern development. Apart from achieving near 100% literacy many years ago, its health statistics are the envy of many far richer countries ... While average income has grown in Cuba [since the Revolution of 1959] at a similar speed to other Latin American countries such as Bolivia, Colombia and El Salvador, the poverty and social conflict experienced in the mainland countries is very apparent. In Cuba, the extremes of opulence and misery are banished in favour of a generalised level of wealth, best described as 'enough to get by'.[38]

The Cuban situation mirrors other efforts to wrestle free of 'Washington Consensus' economics and prioritise the needs of the people. Recent examples of this include Venezuela and Bolivia; like other historical cases, they are closer to radical nationalism than socialism, but Chavez and Morales made strong improvements in health and literacy. A Cuban model of society and democracy is not desirable for Scotland, and we do not consider it socialism in any sense we understand by the term. We refer to the Cuban situation as a thought experiment, for specific purposes, to ask: what if the worst happened?

The truth is that we have plenty of resources to run a just and fair economy in Scotland. Some resources are mobile enough to be bundled out of the country, but most are far from frictionless. Scotland's wind and wave potential, its oil, tourism and whisky industry cannot be shipped off to a lower-wage economy. Strong capital controls and restrictions on finance could help to curtail the freedom of manoeuvre of the ruling classes, just as our present rulers need restrictions on working peoples' freedom, anti-trade union laws and immigration controls.

The ideology of capitalist realism says that we have scarcity, when we have abundant resources to run a civilised society if we redistribute wealth and power. We have none of the restrictions that Cuba began with in the 1950s: thankfully, we are not yet an impoverished colony of the American mafia. If, at the very least, we could replicate Cuba's successes in eliminating the worst of poverty, from our much more developed economic base, we would be further along the right path than we are at present.

Countervailing Power

Improving democracy means more than getting people to vote, or even getting them to vote for better representatives. Even if we make liberal democracy more efficient, it can only aid us in curbing the ultimate source of our democratic deficit, which is capitalist power. As J.K. Galbraith once warned, we are being left with 'private affluence and public squalor'. To advance the interests of the Scottish working class, we must pose the questions of agency and coercion. Who gains from radical policies, and how can we strengthen their influence?

We have already spoken throughout of organised resistance within Scotland. From the handful of landowners who monopolise Scotland's rural landscape, to the business owners who control our electricity and gas and oil, to the financiers in Edinburgh and the middle classes who dominate Holyrood, many vested interests aim to keep Scotland in their command. Any proposal for a 'Nordic model' must confront the coercive power of these interest groups. If Scandinavian economies seem more desirable for everyone, why do so many societies resist this direction?

But beyond these considerations, we need a grasp of *agency*. Who benefits from a radical agenda, and how should they organise? This question will be central to Scottish politics regardless of the result in 2014. Our belief is that present-day alliances in Scotland are shallow and based on a clear absence of long-term strategic vision. The relationship between class, ideology and economic interest is confused. Thus, the Scottish trade unions represent 600,000 working people who have a definite stake in economic change, preserving the welfare state, and demilitarisation. But at Holyrood, they bankroll a party that sits to the right of the Scottish government on almost every issue. How long can this situation sustain itself?

As we discussed in Chapter 4, no political party in Scotland represents a society-wide force for change. Labour and the SNP have pockets of radicalism, and the Left has a large sway over Green policy in Scotland. But no party is the finished article, and no parliamentary alliance has enough will to put redistribution of power and wealth on the agenda. So, at present, everyone who favours change must commit to building broad, extra-parliamentary social movements. This may be joined with parliamentary politics in three ways.

The first is to build cross-party campaigns to defend against the most brutal and unpopular policies. This may involve leadership-level coalition, but the goal is broader: to dismantle tribal boundaries that have no relation to actual disagreements or divergences of interest. In other words, while figureheads stand for these alliances, the aspiration is working relations among grass-roots activists. Thus, the People's Assembly in London was largely dominated by panels of union officials, journalists and elected politicians, but involved a broader ecosystem of campaigners and trade unionists. Radical Independence in Scotland is another example of this. The temptation, of course, is that building the coalition at the top becomes the end rather than the means. In this case, it can strengthen the hand of bureaucratic elements and leaderships at the expense of local initiative.

The second strategy ignores parliamentary and societal leaders. It involves mobilising at community level and building horizontal alliances of activists regardless of party affiliation, as with the Occupy movement and the European and Arab protest movements. These have inspired many imitators, although with declining success, and whether they offer permanent models of opposition to capitalism is not clear. Building horizontal social movements without parties – *bypassing the state* – runs the risk of exhaustion and incorporation. Both of these dangers relate to the inability of spontaneous movements to shake the fundamental structures of wealth and power in society. The state has long ago developed institutions to incorporate dissent.

A third approach is building an anti-capitalist party from scratch. The SSP in Scotland and many similar parties in Europe offered legitimate models, but almost all of these groups seem to collapse amid tribalism or splits. Building a party that is open to grass-roots alliances while remaining principled and disciplined in Parliament has proved tricky. Moreover, right now, building parties in Scotland is liable to lead to frustration and fall-outs, because no single party is capable of monopolising opposition to the market. As a result, the many and varied leftist parties outside Parliament find it difficult to convince ordinary people that they are serious and workable.

In Scotland, as in many other countries, we have two major parties that talk about social justice, but allow social regression in practice. Our aspiration should be an alternative party with a clear agenda for popular economic control and radical democracy, but this party cannot emerge from nowhere. To build alternatives, we must take the lead in forming coalitions and campaigns to defend what we have from attacks.

But most of all, a proper political alternative should not see 'leadership' as gaining admittance to the mystifying cult of parliamentary politics. We should aim to remove the macho aura around political officials, which has been a negative feature of the Scottish Left. Instead, we should see generalising the skills of leadership and political participation as an equal part of our mission, as important in its own way as winning elections. The true democratic alternative lies away from Parliament, on the streets and in workplaces, although this does not mean regressing into the Left's comfort zone of bitterness, jealousy and sectarianism.

Components of a Radical Needs Agenda

The proposals below are not an outline for a perfect society. Rather, we present a sketchy design for transitional institutions and policies designed to prioritise the urgent needs of working-class and oppressed interests in Scottish society. Many proposals go beyond the so-called 'Nordic model', since the social gains of mixed economies can be rolled back without countervailing pressure to press on further. Scandinavia has suffered its own social and democratic recessions, albeit nothing compared to Britain.

We admit to presenting nothing original in this manifesto, which is modelled on the agendas of radical Left parties in Europe, such as Syriza in Greece, Die Linke in Germany, Front de Gauche in France and Left Bloc in Portugal. Leftist movements in the Basque Country and Quebec have also proved influential. These parties have built parliamentary bases just as strong as the SSP in its prime, but have managed to sustain their gains and play a key role in the alternative to the post-2008 crisis. The point is that left-wing radicalism is not isolated to the lunatic fringes, and these demands can attract strong public support. In the case of Syriza, a manifesto like this could command nearly enough support to form a government. Hence, the Left in Scotland does not have to look to UKIP for the model of a parliamentary alternative, as many continue to suggest. We can instead draw on positives examples from across Europe, and the world, that escaped Britain's neoliberal blitzkrieg.

Green New Deal
Scotland has a quarter of Europe's wind and tidal potential, and a tenth of Europe's wave potential. An independent state could play a leading role in meeting the major environmental and economic challenges of the twenty-first century, but decarbonising the economy is too important to be left to corporations and Scotland's landowners. The impediments to

tackling the climate emergency are *social* rather than scientific. Scotland should confront this by committing to a Green New Deal: large-scale infrastructure development projects under the direction of a fully nationalised green economic planning council.[39] A programme developed by the Green New Deal Group (GND) and the Institute for Public Policy Research, have found that we could cut carbon emissions by 80 per cent by 2050 if we enact radical policies today.

This would involve a massive increase in constructing offshore wind and decentralised renewables, such as solar photovoltaics. Another key target is buildings, responsible for 40 per cent of carbon emissions. Building new green homes on a mass scale could solve the crisis of social housing and create tens of thousands of new jobs in construction. These two sectors would form the bulk of the Green New Deal's first investments.

The aim should be to absorb as much of Scotland's economy as possible under this umbrella, to create a subversive precedent for rulers elsewhere. Scotland should treat the war on carbon and pollution with the same urgency that Britain treats a war for oil. Existing subsidies to military industries, and existing military jobs, should be converted to green engineering and investment, backed by a comprehensive retraining program. Every citizen should have the right to work in Scotland's green economy.

According to our calculations, based on the figures offered by GND and projections of Scottish GDP, a Scottish Green New Deal reducing carbon emissions by 80 per cent would cost between £5.63 and £7.94 billion per year, that is, around 4 per cent of GDP. These figures are close to proportionate with Roosevelt's New Deal. It has been estimated that between January 1933 and December 1940 $21.1 billion was spent on public relief and federal works programmes. This amounted to about 3.5 per cent of total GDP over the same period, and today would equal £50 billion annually in the UK or £5 billion plus per year in Scotland.

Nationalise North Sea Oil

The misuse of British North Sea oil revenues was one of the worst economic wastes in history. Norway nationalised 80 per cent of its oil, and used it to secure its people; Britain handed most of it to global corporations, and used the tax receipts to bankroll Thatcher's monetarist experiment, which plunged Scotland into economic darkness. The result is that Norwegians now have a reserve of three quarters of a trillion dollars in its oil fund.

During a phenomenal capitalist crisis, it remains among the most stable economies in the world system.

In Scotland, we could still benefit from nationalisation. Many newspapers downplay the significance of our remaining oil reserves, but moderate estimates suggest at least 24 billion barrels of oil remain in the North Sea. At the present rate, that will return about £1 trillion in tax revenue. But under current rules, we receive just 30 per cent of profits from the extraction and sale of oil, while 70 per cent is taken by multinational corporations. According to Ralph Blake, an analyst in the Scottish financial industry and former head of research and strategy in investment banking, we could triple our revenues if we nationalise North Sea oil.[40] And that is if we accept a conservative estimate for the future price of oil – $110 per barrel for the next four years. This figure is 15–25 per cent lower than the forecasts estimated by the Department of Energy and Climate Change ($130) and the OECD ($150).

But Scotland does need to diversify, rather than rely on this polluting and outdated energy source as an economic crutch. Whatever happens with North Sea oil ownership, we must make sure the resource is used to fund Scotland's comparative advantage in the new Green economy.

Scottish Currency

Scotland, say SNP leaders, can stabilise after independence by remaining within a 'currency union'. But we already belong to the Sterling union, and it has been a poor deal for the Scottish economy. British monetary policy has subordinated industry to finance, and centralised power in the South of England. We suffered the brunt of this in the 1980s, and the 'readjustment' of our economy along financial lines came at the expense of the manufacturing working class. Examples like Greece and Ireland show further dangers of a currency union on the terms of the stronger state. We should use our natural and human wealth to set up an independent currency and a different economic model. This has worked for countries like Norway and Denmark, two of the richest economies in Europe, and it can work for Scotland.[41] A new Scottish currency will allow us to adopt flexible policies which break from the US-UK model and deliver wealth redistribution.

Finance People Not Profit

In the short run, public-sector investment funds, including pensions, must invest in the low-carbon economy in Scotland or face penalties. The legal separation of investment and commercial banking should also be enforced. In the medium term, we should centralise as much as possible within a national investment bank charged with clear Green objectives. On an international scale, we should champion the Tobin Tax on world financial transactions to pay for poverty alleviation in Africa. It has been estimated that this minimal tax (0.1 per cent tax on the sale or purchase of currencies) would produce a yield of at least $150 billion annually.[42] In the long term, we need to work towards the nationalisation of all investment, forcing finance to fund the local economy, particularly the Green economy.

Progressive Taxation and Redistribution

The UK has a regressive taxation system: the poor pay more of their income to the government than the rich, once we account for indirect taxes. We should aim to reverse this huge injustice. VAT, a horrific Thatcherite tax that targets the poorest, should be scrapped, and replaced with fairer taxes on income and property. Inherited wealth, which serves to perpetuate elites across generations, must be a particular target. Existing levies are weak, and accountants refer to it as a 'voluntary tax' because so many avoidance loopholes exist, so we should have much stiffer inheritance taxes. Taxation, at present, is used to redistribute money from the poorest to the richest; if Scotland abandons the US-UK model, we should abandon this topsy-turvy order. This also means scrapping any commitment to low corporation tax. If cheap business rates and minimal labour rights made an economy dynamic, present-day Scotland would be Europe's workshop. We need to increase income tax for the biggest earners, and also introduce new taxes on wealth and land. Even introducing modest wealth, land and property taxes would increase annual revenue by more than £1 billion in Scotland.[43]

End All Privatisation – Renationalise Infrastructure

Has the UK experiment in extreme privatisation made the economy more efficient? Ask train users: every day they see evidence that Thatcher's fire sale has been a costly debacle. Subordinating vital resources like energy to shareholder profits, rather than the long-term needs for Green investment, is a callous exercise in short-termism. At present, the resources of Scottish people are often owned by overseas corporations. Meanwhile, the Labour experiment in the private financing of hospitals, schools and just about everything else has been an economic disaster. Private profits should have no role in the provision of basic needs. We should seek to reverse the trends of the past decades, and bring our resources under the democratic control of the people.

The madness of railway privatisation indicates some of its worst features.[44] Not only has it been an economic disaster, it also been widely acknowledged to have damaged safety, as evidenced by the Hatfield disaster in 2000 in which four people died and seventy were injured. The railways, along with other key sectors of the economy, need to be brought back into public ownership.

Free Childcare, Equal Pay, Maternity Leave

A quarter of the average British family budget goes on childcare costs – double that of France and three times that of Germany. Britain also ranks as the second worst country in Europe for maternity and paternity leave, with new parents receiving less than ten weeks' paid time-off. At present, the independence case is floundering because it cannot convince women to vote Yes. We should enshrine commitments to free childcare, equal pay and rights for mothers in the Scottish Constitution.

Fund Education

If we want a more egalitarian Scotland, radical steps must be taken to reform the education system. Education should equalise opportunities, giving every child an equal chance to succeed. But the current system entrenches inequality, rather than alleviating it.

Research shows that kids from working-class families are disadvantaged from the first day of primary school.[45] Differences in attainment widen significantly throughout primary and secondary school. As a result, 60 per cent of young entrants to Scottish universities in 2011–12 had parents from managerial and professional occupations compared to only 20 per cent from working-class families.[46]

According to the charity Save the Children, the biggest factors leading to attainment inequalities in Scottish schools are pervasive levels of poverty and deprivation. This, they show, not only leads to grade inequalities, but also affects children's development: 'Children born into poverty are four times as likely as children from the most affluent backgrounds to have developmental difficulties.'[47]

As well as enacting a serious poverty-reduction strategy, a new Scottish state needs to overhaul the education system. Funding should be increased at a pre-school level as well as for primary, secondary and tertiary education. From an early age, every child should have the right to one-on-one support from qualified teachers acting as personal tutors. This would ensure that no one falls behind children from advantaged backgrounds. Proper funding and resourcing of nurseries and schools would end the current situation where over-stretched teachers cannot find time to support learners, while recently qualified teachers struggle to find a job. This sort of policy works. A clear example is Finland, which provides large levels of funding for one-to-one support. Numerous studies show that Finland has both the highest performing and most equal education system in the world.[48]

Equality and Discrimination

Scotland should make a commitment to eradicating discrimination and exclusion of women and minorities. There should be a 50 per cent quota for parties standing for Holyrood election, to enforce equality in representation; this should also apply to the boards of every private and public company in Scotland. Moreover, this should apply as a general principle, involving racial, religious and sexual minorities as well.

Exit from US-UK Military Alliances

Scotland contributes £3.3 billion to annual UK defence spending,[49] but an independent nation needs just a fraction of this. This money should be redirected into poverty alleviation programs and funding for a Green New Deal, and we should commit to world peace and internationalism in the Scottish Constitution. The opportunity to cut military spending after the Cold War has been lost. NATO, in its present form, is a systematic extension of an American aim to isolate Russia in Europe and, in recent decades, in Asia; this tactic is destabilising the global system and has everything to do with power games and nothing to do with 'security'. Scotland should work with other nation states and social movements outside the orbit of Anglo-American imperialism to win the case for a global reduction in arms spending. All arms trading on Scottish soil should be banned.

Scrap Trident

At present, we are sleepwalking into spending £80 billion on a replacement for the Trident nuclear weapons system, supported, to varying degrees, by a cross-party Westminster consensus. This horrific waste of money is the very epitome of everything a humane economic strategy should oppose. Moreover, a huge swathe of Scottish society stands dead against it. An independent Scotland should not waver in its commitment to abolishing Trident and fighting for a nuclear-free planet.

Working-Class Power
At present, defending the rights of poor people by solidarity strike action is illegal, while the right of rich people to defend their property by all measures of force is enshrined in law. We need to reverse this injustice. Scotland should abolish the anti-trade union laws that criminalise solidarity, and give workers the right to strike on political grounds – a basic democratic freedom – to reverse the worst of Britain's settlement. Beyond this, Scotland should give workers the legal right to veto management decisions by a simple majority vote, and allow workers to assume control over companies as cooperatives.

Empowered Participatory Governance
Modelled on Porto Allegre, we should move towards direct involvement of government service users of the lowest socio-economic strata in administration and political decision making. In particular, council-level economic decisions should be made by neighbourhood assemblies; representative democracy, that is, local politicians, should work to embrace and support participatory governance.

Land Reform
In a very immediate sense, the right of tenants and communities to buy land *against the wishes of landlords* must be put in law. In the medium term, we need a commitment to break up the feudal land structure. If land reform cannot be secured by voluntary means, the state should intervene to protect against landlord infringements. The Scottish state should make definite and firm commitments to redistribute land according to agreed targets. This may be achieved by placing punitive wealth taxes on large landowners, who are an unproductive drain on the economy.

Maximum Working Week
Britain has far lower productivity than nations such as France, but retains the illusion of rising living standards because people work longer hours. The result is twofold. One, it means that Britain is one of the worst places in Europe for family life and has among the worst rates of stress, depression and mental illness. Two, it works to reduce the chances of employment for many people. So-called 'free choice' is leading to a miserable and

unequal society. Scotland should set the maximum working week to 35 hours, to allow for more leisure time, as well as greater civic and political participation. Government should work with unions to make sure no loss of pay results.

Substantive Measures of Economic Progress
Scotland should abolish gross national product as a measure of economic performance. We should adopt a 'composite index of human progress' (personal development, social cohesion, social justice, respect for the environment). This is based on research which shows that equal countries have the highest achievements in terms of all social measures, from mental health and crime to reported happiness.

Freedom of Movement for People, not Money
We should stop worrying about the 'brain drain' in Scotland, and instead worry about the brain gain. Talented people across the world face discrimination and persecution in their own country and want somewhere to live and work in freedom. We should give them a home. We should reverse the huge injustices of 'Fortress Britain', and the mindless tide of anti-immigrant propaganda, and set a humane example for the rest of the world. This would be a true internationalism, a world away from 'British jobs for British workers'.

Afterword:
After the White Paper, After Britain

In late November 2013, Alex Salmond and Nicola Sturgeon launched the long-awaited White Paper on independence. For years, the nationalist faithful had anticipated Scotland's answer to the Declaration of Independence, the Magna Carta and the Rights of Man and Citizen. Salmond promised, with only marginally less pomp, that the White Paper would be Scotland's greatest document since 1320.[1] Yes enthusiasts counted the days before the launch, which would mark, they felt, the real beginning of the 2014 debate, and the triumph of bold SNP leadership. Unionists also had a lot resting on the White Paper, foreseeing their chance to sink independence forever.

Ultimately, neither side could claim victory. The document was short on messianic declarations, and long in detail, aiming once again to reassure sceptics with continuity in everything from NATO, sterling and the EU, to television, university applications and vehicle licensing. Salmond and Sturgeon, as Alex Massie noted, pitched the question as 'why not independence?'[2] They did not outline an overarching vision of twenty-first-century citizenship. The document was competent, as unionist pundits admitted, but unspectacular. Even sympathetic columnists conceded a glaring omission: yes, independence is workable, but if stasis is our goal, why bother voting Yes? To this extent, the White Paper was not the qualitative shift nationalists wanted.

Nevertheless, compared to Yes Scotland's launch, there was evidence they had listened on the gender front. By putting Salmond and Sturgeon on equal billing, they broke with male-dominated panels; more importantly, they promised 30 hours a week of free childcare. Critics claimed, with some justification, that these policies were achievable with existing Holyrood powers. 'This has nothing to do with independence,' snapped *Scotsman* columnist Bill Jamieson, 'but in seeking to conflate independence with specific financial benefits for a targeted group of voters it has reduced a profound constitutional issue to the level of retail politics.'[3] But Jamieson misses the point. Sturgeon's proposals forced a symbolic break with the unreformed, masculine approach to citizenship inherited from Westminster. The UK has the eighth worst gender pay gap of 27 EU countries, and full equality is not expected until 2067.[4] Developed societies could, and should, declare the right to nursery subsidies, along with free education and housing, as basic citizen rights. Scotland, like Britain, owns the resources to fulfil these obligations and more.

Of course, such promises assume, with respect to the Yes movement, that the SNP retains full sovereignty, reserving sole rights to break its own rules. They forbade, remember, any post-independence policies from official Yes communications. Here, by contrast, Salmond and Sturgeon promised goodies galore. As leaders of a governing party, perhaps this is their prerogative. Yet having conceded exceptions, it opens the question of broader citizen rights. The White Paper's oversights are peculiar: if free childcare is a legitimate promise, why not end anti-union laws, introduce a green new deal, or renationalise rail and energy? The document paraded an SNP vision, which Salmond never denied. But, by blurring the lines between election policies and citizen manifesto, it left a nagging sensation of a missed opportunity. They toyed with bold statecraft, and then closed up the box again.

Better Together's response was sullen, as expected. Their principle criticism, that Britain could deny Scotland access to a sterling currency zone, suggested a bully's charter. It followed a pattern: weeks earlier, Labour Govan MP Ian Davidson had pleaded with BAE Systems, a major Clydeside employer, to repatriate military jobs to England if Scotland votes Yes.[5] Davidson, we were to understand, preferred to pauperise his own constituents than accept Scottish sovereignty. Likewise, Alistair Darling, George Osborne and David Cameron would rather risk the livelihoods of two nations than admit the possibility of a fair trading agreement between independent states.

Although our vision of independence rejects arms production and sterling zones, we regard Westminster's strong-arm tactics as the lowest form of manipulation. But then, perhaps we have no right to be outraged. After all, the UK state always rules by fear and state of emergency, as we have explained throughout this book. Their approach to independence follows an established formula, where apocalyptic scenarios and wild-eyed threats have hectored British people into invading Iraq, imposing austerity and privatising their social inheritance.

Grass-roots unionist reactions ranged from the flaky to the bizarre. Mike Dailly, Better Together's token anti-poverty campaigner, rejected Salmond's depictions of Britain as unequal. He argued that measuring inequality by the GINI coefficient is inaccurate, since it only covers income inequality, and by other measures Britain is doing fine, as shown by 'the UK's first class National Health Service, local authority public services, and access to schools, housing, colleges and university education'. Dailly also insisted the UK had the 'fourth highest ... growth in net disposable household income in 2012'.[6]

Even taking Dailly's advice, and ignoring the GINI coefficient, Britain fails on a range of more substantive measures. In social terms, the UK wealth gap is twice as wide as in any other EU state.[7] In geographical terms, poor regions of the UK have average incomes of £11,000, compared to £111,000 for the richest, a tenfold gap.[8] Britain's wage decline since 2010, the period lauded by Dailly, was the fourth worst of 27 EU countries.[9] The UK has the second gravest fuel poverty in Europe (ahead of Estonia),[10] the third highest housing costs,[11] one of the lowest state pensions,[12] the fourth poorest elderly people,[13] and the highest infant mortality of all western European countries. Our Dickensian levels of childhood deprivation, according to the World Health Organization, are a Westminster 'policy choice', not an accident.[14]

As for the NHS, Westminster is dismantling everything unique and laudable, while importing worst practice from elsewhere. Local authority public services are not particular to Britain, but our regions face higher than average austerity, due to our low tax, pro-market regime. University fees of £9,000, and free schools, are stripping the core principles of comprehensive education. Britain's housing crisis is notorious, thanks to council house sales, property bubbles and the bedroom tax. Most of all, amid global neoliberalism, the UK was a vanguard state, scouring all principles of social justice from public policy. UK inequality rose by 32 per cent between 1960 and 2005.[15] By comparison, it increased by just 23 per cent in the US, despite decades of Nixon, Ford, Reagan and Clinton's 'New Democrats'. In Sweden, inequality fell by 12 per cent.[16] These are the arrangements that Dailly, styling himself as a poverty campaigner, seeks to defend. His arguments would carry more weight if he admitted the problems, but argued for a Westminster, Labour solution. Instead, he maintains full denial of the facts, and champions the UK being used as a Petri dish for neoliberal experiments.

Social Citizenship

The White Paper could never answer every query from Better Together, because many problems stem from the framing of the debate. No one expects Alistair Darling to guarantee Britain's economic security, or to specify new powers for Scotland, or even to forbid another Iraq. Salmond and Sturgeon presented aspirations, a platform for future SNP government, more than a blueprint. While critics can ruminate on the document's workability, they cannot insist on clarifying each footnote prior to a Yes vote. Never has a developed nation's vote for independence led to an economic crash or isolation from international institutions. Poorer, weaker countries than Scotland have ceded from multinational units without incurring doomsday. Scottish policy-makers have distinct advantages, including the precedent of more than 150 states attaining sovereignty in the twentieth century. None of them had a fleshed-out design for statehood beforehand. Since the White Paper could not resolve every niggle, its success must be judged by its air of competence. To this degree, it received pass marks.

But it still suffers from strategic inertia. Salmond and Sturgeon got stuck between reassuring bromides and imagining a better social order. Their hesitant critique of Britain's failings left them buffeted between these two messages. Throughout this book, we have linked the UK's neo-imperial project – as financial haven, arms manufacturer and leading American client – to neoliberal morality, privatisation policies and social regression. Post-war Britain was no socialist utopia, and we have no wish to romanticise the Attlee era, far less Wilson's technocratic modernism, or Callaghan's meek surrender. But in this era of chav-bashing, hooting Hooray Henrys, asset-stripping and austerity, an element of decency went missing. Earlier governments committed to eradicating the evils of squalor, ignorance, want, idleness and disease, to install the building-blocks of a just social order. As goals of national pride, no citizen should sleep on the streets, or die from preventable diseases, or reach the age of 16 unable to read and write. Whether these were dreams or real aspirations is debatable. But today, policy imaginations are held captive by neoliberal conformity, hence the failure to envision social citizenship.

If Scotland votes Yes, it will be the second new European state to emerge in the twenty-first century, after Montenegro. To justify this status, independence must explain its purpose. While the former Yugoslavia was in a state of unavoidable collapse after the Cold War, the US-UK order remains the dominant world power. Iraq and Lehmann Brothers damaged the intellectual credibility of Pentagon supremacy and Wall Street economics, and 1990s stridency may never return. Today, who claims history has ended? But prising hegemonic alliances apart is a global task. Scotland's independence must recover a sense of history: rejecting the illusions of the last epoch, we must reinvigorate justice, rights and responsibilities. A blueprint for victory needs greater ambition; it must restore, overhaul and improve what we have lost since the Thatcher-Reagan coup.

What would reasserting social citizenship mean in practice? As T.H. Marshall explained, 'What matters is that there is a general enrichment of the concrete substance of civilized life, a general reduction of risk and insecurity, an equalization between the more and the less fortunate at every level – between the healthy and the sick, the employed and the unemployed, the old and the active, the bachelor and the father of a large family'.[17] We believe these aims make an agreeable clash with everything Britain symbolises. They are aspirations; but worthwhile aspirations, a framework for radical renewal, without constituting a socialist utopia.

In Marshall's era, the 1950s, it seemed inevitable that social values would prevail over the grubby inheritances of private privilege, aristocracy, elitism, violence, ignorance and tyranny. But the last four decades taught us that justice is not predestined and rights must be seized, or they will be withdrawn. In intellectual terms, a cult of individualism and markets colonised public policy and eradicated critical views. No amount of evidence disproves the inevitability of austerity, rail privatisation, or workfare, because, apparently, 'there is no alternative'. In moral terms, riches and breeding become synonymous with personal worth, while poverty becomes a disease, caused by individual failings, whether these be corruption, laziness, or biological inferiority. Policy-makers grew accustomed and habituated to free market solutions, regardless of their own beliefs. Thus, Scotland's main parties and leading intellectuals are not enthusiasts for border controls, the bedroom tax, racialised policing, energy fatcats, Made in Chelsea, or Eton snobbery. They are not cruel people; but they enforce a system that perpetuates these mindless cruelties.

Social citizenship is not destined to triumph, but in 2014, it has an opening. No Westminster election, as we have explained, will ever allow us the right to reject nuclear alliances, the arms trade, an elitist state and voodoo economics. These are the true stakes, and we should be unabashed about explaining them.

In private moments, Better Together leaders refer to themselves as 'project fear'.[18] Yes spokespeople, including Nicola Sturgeon, have made considerable capital from this confession. The term is apt, in a sense, because Darling et al. comprise the spearhead of neoliberal ideas in British society, and they enforce conformity by spreading panic. Radical economics has been scoured from public policy for decades, using this same formula. But the admission proves nothing, since stoking fears is, after all, their privilege. It works for them. The question is, what does Yes Scotland substitute for permanent emergency?

So far, SNP strategy may be termed 'project optimism'. Optimism is a cognitive stance, disciplining oneself to assume that things will improve, that better days are just around the corner, regardless of appearances, because we are the best, and the best will be rewarded.[19] Just like panic, these ideas involve cult-like obedience, as shown by their spread, from the US, in the last four decades. As we explained in Chapter 5, the scientific evidence for applying this to politics is dubious. While leaders may exude optimism – as do Salmond and Sturgeon – there are no guarantees it will spread, osmosis-like, to the public. Projecting confidence is a virtue; but confidence in what?

Optimism and hope are not the same. Hope, though, does link our fate to our actions, and such formulas are the missing ingredients from the referendum. We are not guaranteed to prevail over the homogenising dirty politics of Westminster. But in 2014, we can insist on a better way. Social citizenship, the reduction of risk, the sharing of burdens, the instincts of care and responsibility are workable principles of public policy. They endured during Britain's most successful decades of growth; they continue, to varying degrees, in similar northern European economies, which have higher taxation, lower inequality and better living standards. We are not fated to walk Westminster's path.

As socialists, we reject unequal wages, inherited property and imperialist rivalries on basic principles of justice. But we also accept that these are divisive principles. What Scots can unite upon is the unsustainable direction of British capitalism. If we vote No, we all but guarantee more decades of austerity, privatisation and warfare. We will miss our chance to contribute a working model of environmental sustainability. We will assume, with utmost complacency, that Labour governments are capable of reforming Westminster, despite all evidence to the contrary. Let us not repeat our mistakes of 1979, and resign ourselves to more Thatcher decades. Our vote counts. By our actions we can restore hope, assert cooperation and tolerance, and deliver a message: that Scotland will never again submit to the administration of mindless cruelty.

Notes

Introduction

1. T. Blair, *A Journey*, London: Arrow Books, p. 650.
2. Ibid., p. 251.
3. Ibid., p. 651.
4. R. Wilkinson and K. Pickett, *The Spirit Level: Why Equality is Better for Everyone*, London: Penguin, 2010.
5. R. Hahnel, *The ABCs of Political Economy: A Modern Approach*, London: Pluto Press, 2002, p. 279.
6. M. Hilson, *The Nordic Model*, London: Reaktion, 2008, pp. 184, emphasis added.
7. D. Simpson, 'An Environment for Economic Growth: Is Small Still Beautiful?', in D. MacKay (ed.), *Scotland's Economic Future*, Edinburgh: Reform Scotland, 2008, p. 30, emphasis added.
8. 'World Economic Outlook Database, October 2013' IMF [online], 8 October 2013 <http://www.imf.org/external/pubs/ft/weo/2013/02/weodata/index.aspx>.
9. L. Bews, 'Rich are 270 Times Better Off Than Poor', *Daily Record*, 20 June 2013.
10. 'Unions Must Stay True', *Daily Record*, 24 April 2012.
11. J. Mitchell, L. Bennie and R. Johns, *The Scottish National Party: Transition to Power*, Oxford: Oxford University Press, 2012, p. 65.
12. S. Boggan, 'Election '97 – Patriotic Blair Sets Out Global Vision', *Independent*, 22 April 1997.
13. K. Farquharson, 'Cultural Revolution as SNP Learns to Love the Brits', *Scotland on Sunday*, 18 March 2012.
14. N. Ascherson, *Stone Voices*, London: Granta, 2002, p. 237.
15. W.L. Miller, 'The Death of Unionism?', in T.M. Devine (ed.), *Scotland and the Union 1707–2007*, Edinburgh: Edinburgh University Press, 2008, p. 183.
16. I. Bell, 'When the Scots and English Both Want to be Less British', *Herald Scotland*, 18 May 2013.
17. Ibid.

Chapter 1   Endgame Britain? The Four Crises of 'Anglobalisation'

1. B. Brogan, 'It's Time to Celebrate the Empire, Says Brown', *Daily Mail*, 15 January 2005.

2. N. Ferguson, *Empire: How Britain Made the Modern World*, London: Penguin, 2003; N. Ferguson, *Colossus: The Rise and Fall of the American Empire*, London: Penguin, 2004.

3. M. Davis, *Late Victorian Holocausts: El Niño Famines and the Making of the Third World*, London: Verso, 2001, p. 9.

4. Ferguson, *Empire: How Britain Made the Modern World*, p. 240.

5. D. Stewart, "A Complex Question About the Remnants of Empire': The Labour Party and the Falklands War' in B. Frank, C. Horner, and D. Stewart (eds), *The British Labour Movement and Imperialism*, Newcastle: Cambridge Scholars, 2010.

6. This is how Colin Gray, a senior strategist in the Reagan administration, described the military relationship between the US and Britain: C.S. Gray, *Another Bloody Century: Future Warfare*, Penang: Phoenix Press, 2007, p. 77.

7. Robert Cooper, *The Breaking of Nations: Order and Chaos in the Twenty-First Century*, New York: Atlantic Press.

8. N. Mann, 'Blair says Britain is "force for good"', *BBC* [online], 5 January 2002 < http://news.bbc.co.uk/1/hi/uk_politics/1743985.stm >.

9. A. McSmith, *No Such Thing as Society*, London: Constable and Robinson, 2010.

10. 'Blair's Statement in Full', *Telegraph*, 18 March 2003.

11. P. Beaumont and J. Walters, 'Greenspan Admits Iraq Was About Oil, as Deaths Put at 1.2m', *Observer*, 16 September 2007.

12. T. Shipman, 'Labour MP Calls to Abolish Britain's Multi-billion-pound Arms Industry Are Met With Ridicule', *Daily Mail*, 16 September 2013.

13. R. Burn-Callander, 'Cessation Of Iraq Hostilities Hits BAE Systems', *Management Today*, 16 February 2012.

14. 'The SIPRI Top 100 Arms-producing and Military Services Companies in the World Excluding China, 2011' *Stockholm International Peace Research Institute*, Stockholm: SIPRI, 2013.

15. S. Johnson, 'Britain's Enemies Will "Exploit Scottish independence to Cut UK Power"', *Telegraph*, 17 October 2012.

16. S. Johnson, 'UK "a World Power in Irreversible Decline" if Scotland Separates', *Telegraph*, 1 May 2013.

17. E. Londoño, 'Iraq, Afghan Wars Will Cost $4 Trillion to $6 Trillion, Harvard Study Says', *Washington Post*, 28 March 2013.

18. 'Afghanistan and Iraq "Have Cost Taxpayers £20bn"', *Telegraph*, 20 June 2010.

19. I. Dale, 'In Conversation with Alex Salmond', *Total Politics*, 1 August 2008, emphasis added.

20. G. Newey, 'Ten Myths About Thatcher', *London Review of Books*, 17 April 2013.

21. R. Middleton, *Government Versus the Market: Growth of the Public Sector, Economic Management and British Economic Performance, 1890–1979*, Cheltenham: Edward Elgar, 1997, p. 630.

22. G. Newey, 'Ten Myths About Thatcher', *London Review of Books*, 17 April 2013.

23. R. Blackburn, 'The Ruins of Westminster', *New Left Review*, I/191 (January–February 1992).

24. B. Clift, and J. Tomlinson, 'Whatever Happened to the Balance of Payments "Problem"? The Contingent (re-)construction of British Economic Performance Assessment', *British Journal of Politics and International Relations*, Vol. 10, No. 4 (November 2008).

25. H.J. Chang, *23 Things They Don't Tell You About Capitalism*, New York: Bloomsbury, 2010, p. 19.

26. G. Turner, *The Credit Crunch: Housing Bubbles, Globalisation and the Worldwide Economic Crisis*, London: Pluto Press, 2008, p. 26.

27. P. Anderson, 'Homeland', *New Left Review*, II/81 (May–June 2013), pp. 22–3.

28. L. Elliott and D. Atkinson, 'Talk is Cheap', *Guardian*, 18 May 2007.

29. P. Hitchens, *The Cameron Delusion*, London: Continuum, 2010, p. 122.

30. 'UK Politics: Tony Blair's Speech in Full', *BBC* [online], 28 September 1999 < http://news.bbc.co.uk/1/hi/uk_politics/460009.stm >.

31. T. Newburn, and R. Reiner, 'Crime and Penal Policy', in Seldon, A. (ed.). *Blair's Britain, 1997–2007*, Cambridge: Cambridge University Press, 2007, p. 319.

32. P. Toynbee, 'Equal Opportunity is Fantasy in Any Society This Unequal', *Guardian*, 20 July 2009.

33. S. Lansley, 'Why Economic Inequality Leads to Collapse', *Guardian*, 5 February 2012.

34. O. Jones, *Chavs: The Demonisation of the Working Class*, London: Verso, 2012, p. 97.

35. Ibid.

36. L. Eliott, 'UK Unemployment Falls', *Guardian*, 12 June 2013.

37. Ibid.

38. A. Gentlemen, 'UK's Bedroom Tax and Housing Crisis Threaten Human Rights, Says UN Expert', *Guardian*, 11 September 2013.

39. E. Dugan, 'Summer of Hunger: Huge Rise in Food Bank Use as Demand Linked to "Welfare Reform"', *Independent*, 9 August 2013.

40. R. Wilkinson and K. Pickett, *The Spirit Level: Why Equality is Better for Everyone*, London: Penguin, 2009.

41. 'Ed Miliband: It Would Be "Politically Crackers" to Spend Like the Last Labour Government', *New Statesman* [online], 5 September 2012 < http://www.newstatesman.com/blogs/politics/2012/09/ed-miliband-it-would-be-politically-crackers-spend-last-labour-government >.

42. P. Krugman, 'Holy Coding Error, Batman', *New York Times* [online], 16 April 2013.

43. W. Hutton, *Them and Us*, London: Penguin, 2011.

44. Jones, *Chavs. The Demonization of the Working Class*, p. 214.

45. Scottish Social Attitudes Survey, 2010, UK Data Service.

46. 'Blind Justice', *Economist*, 4 May 2013.

47. J. Ford Rojas, 'London Riots: Lidl Water Thief Jailed for Six Months', *Telegraph*, 11 August 2011.

48. F. Forsyth, 'One Law for the Rich, Quite Another for the Poor', *Express*, 6 July 2012.

49. P. Norris, *Democratic Deficit: Critical Citizens Revisited*, Cambridge: Cambridge University Press, 2011, p. 71.

50. W. Hutton, *Them and Us*, London: Penguin, 2011, p. 182.

51. R. Syal, J. Treanor and N. Mathiason, 'City's Influence Over Conservatives Laid Bare by Research Into Donations', *Guardian*, 30 September 2011.

52. P. Mair, 'Partyless Democracy', *New Left Review*, II/2 (March–April 2000).

53. Ibid.

54. D. McBride, 'It's "Lord" Cowell', *Daily Mail*, 20 September 2013.

55. House of Commons Library, 'UK Election Statistics', Research Paper 03/59, London: Social and General Statistics Section, 1 July 2003.

56. M. Förster, 'Divided We Stand: Why Inequality Keeps Rising', *OECD*, December 2011.

57. *Panorama*, 'Britain on the Brink: Back to the 70s?', BBC, 9 July 2012.

Chapter 2   British Nationalism: The Missing Link

1. D. Willets, 'England and Britain, Europe and the Anglosphere', in A. Gamble and T. Wright (eds), *Britishness*, Cambridge: Wiley-Blackwell, 2009, p. 57.

2. T. Nairn, (1971) 'British Nationalism and the EEC', *New Left Review*, I/69 (September–October 1971).

3. S. Johnson, 'Johann Lamont: Referendum a Chance to Dispel "Virus" of Nationalism', *Telegraph*, 22 September 2013.

4. N. Davidson, *The Origins of Scottish Nationhood*, London: Pluto, 2000, p. 4.

5. G. Eaton, 'Why is Nigel Farage on Question Time So Often?', *New Statesman*, 13 June 2013.

6. J. Delingpole, 'Nigel Farage – the Only Politician Who Dares Say What We're Thinking', *Telegraph*, 20 September 2013.

7. 'UKIP Leader Nigel Farage Likens Scottish Nationalism Campaign to Fascism After Protesters Storm His Press Conference', *Daily Record*, 17 May 2013.

8. G. Galloway, 'Scotland, Nigel and Me', *Red Molucca* [online], 19 May 2013 <http://redmolucca.wordpress.com/2013/05/19/scotland-farage-and-me/>.

9. J. Maxwell, 'Anti-Englishness and the SNP', *New Statesman*, 2 April 2012.

10. 'Anger as Labour Lord Likens Alex Salmond to Italian Fascist Leader Mussolini', *Scotsman*, 2 December 2009.

11. S. Carrell, 'Labour MP Tom Harris Forced to Resign as Social Media Tsar', *Guardian*, 16 January 2012.

12. J. Lewis, 'Scottish Secretary Moore Talks of "Parallels" Between SNP and UKIP Campaigns', *Herald Scotland*, 17 September 2013.

13. N. Watt and S. Carrell, 'Nigel Farage and Alex Salmond Trade Insults in Battle of Nationalists', *Guardian*, 17 May 2013.

14. W. Bain, 'Alex Salmond? Progressive?', *Guardian*, 24 January 2012.

15. T. Nairn, (1971) 'British Nationalism and the EEC', *New Left Review*, I/69 (September–October 1971).

16. M. Billig, 'Nationalism and Richard Rorty: The Text as a Flag for Pax Americana', *New Left Review*, Vol. I/202 (November–December 1993).

17. M. Billig, *Banal Nationalism*, London: Sage, 1995, p. 55.

18. G. Orwell, 'Notes on Nationalism', *Orwell Prize* [online], 1945 <http://theorwellprize.co.uk/george-orwell/by-orwell/essays-and-other-works/notes-on-nationalism/>.

19. J. Freedland, 'London 2012: We've Glimpsed Another Kind of Britain, So Let's Fight For It', *Guardian*, 10 August 2012.

20. 'If You Felt That the 2015 UK General Election Would Result in a Conservative-led Government, How Likely or Unlikely Would You Be to Vote for Independence?', *What Scotland Thinks* [online], October 2012 <http://whatscotlandthinks.org/questions/if-conservative-led-uk-government-in-2015-likelyunlikely-to-vote-for-independen#table>.

21. 'Minister Quits Over Fire "Fascist's" Row', *BBC* [online], 26 November 2002 <http://news.bbc.co.uk/1/hi/scotland/2513847.stm>.

22. A. Travis, 'Virginity Tests for Immigrants "Reflected Dark Age Prejudices" of 1970s Britain', *Guardian*, 8 May 2011.

23. V. Brignell, 'The Eugenics Movement Britain Wants to Forget', *New Statesman*, 9 December 2010.

24. G. Walker, *Thomas Johnson: Lives of the Left*, Manchester: Manchester University Press, 1988, p. 67.

25. Ibid., p. 82

26. R.M. Douglas, 'The British Left, Colonies, and International Trusteeship', in R.M. Douglas, M.D. Callahan and E. Bishop (eds), *Imperialism on Trial: International Oversight of Colonial Rule in Historical Perspective*, Oxford: Lexington Books, 2006, p. 160.

27. N. Watt, 'Howard Flight Echoes Keith Joseph's 1974 Warning That "Our Human Stock is Threatened"', *Guardian*, 25 November 2010.

28. 'Life Sentence for Sighthill Killer', *Guardian*, 14 December 2001.

29. S. Johnson, 'Record Number of "Racist" Attacks on English in Scotland', *Telegraph*, 11 December 2012.

30. 'Don't Hate the English', *Daily Record*, 12 December 2012.

31. Scottish Government, 'Racist Incidents Recorded by the Police in Scotland, 2011–12' [online], 2012 <http://www.scotland.gov.uk/Publications/2012/12/4963>.

32. I. Bell, 'When the Scots and English Both Want to be Less British', *Herald Scotland*, 18 May 2013

33. 'Church's "Powell-style Racism" Against Irish', *Scotsman*, 9 April 2002.

34. Ibid.

35. G.P.T. Finn, 'Prejudice in the History of Irish Catholics in Scotland', Paper to the 24th History Workshop Conference, Glasgow Caledonian University, 1990, pp. 5–6.

36. S. Cosgrove, 'The Humble Potato Has Caused a New Rise in Stupidity', *Daily Record*, 13 May 2004.

37. P. Mac GiollaBhain, 'It's Still Not Easy Being Irish in Scotland', *Guardian*, 13 April 2011.

38. K. McKenna, 'Scotland Should Thank the English Settlers', *Observer*, 23 December 2012.

39. H. Trevor-Roper, *The Invention of Scotland: Myth and History*, New Haven, CT: Yale University Press, 2008.

Chapter 3   Caledonia PLC: Capitalist Power in Scotland

1. E. Barnes and A. Whittaker, 'Scottish Independence: New Poll Gives Yes Camp Hope', *Scotland on Sunday*, 16 September 2013.

2. 'Will Scotland Prosper?', *Daily Express*, 19 February 1979.

3. 'No Sudden Rise in Living Standards on Independence', *Herald Scotland*, 23 April 2013.

4. J. Brown, 'Imagine a Feudal Country Where 432 Families Own Half the Land. Welcome to Scotland', *Independent*, 1 August 2013.

5. D. McCrone, *Understanding Scotland: The Sociology of a Nation*, London: Routledge, 2001, p.125.

6. W. Hutton, *Them and Us*, London: Abacus, 2011, p. 152.

7. I. Johnston, 'Scotland 2004: Why We've Never Had it So Good', *Scotsman*, 15 May 2004.

8. G. McCrone, *Scottish Independence: Weighing up the Economics*, Edinburgh: Birlinn, 2013, p. 74.

9. K. Skeoch, 'The Scottish Financial Services Sector After the Global Financial Crisis: Celtic Eagle, Sparrow, Lion, or Hare?', in D. MacKay (ed.), *Scotland's Economic Future*, Edinburgh: Reform Society, 2011.

10. 'Financial Industry: Industry Facts', *Industrial Spotlight* [online] <http://www.industryspotlight.org.uk/financial/industry-facts.php>.

11. 'Financial Services Overview', *Scottish Development International*, 8 October 2010.

12. A. Darling, 'Dialogues Concerning the Banking Crisis: The Hume Lecture 2011', David Hume Institute Occasional Paper No. 91, 2011.

13. L. Riddoch, 'Time to Work Out Our Own New Deal', *The Scotsman*, 2 July 2012.

14. S. Boyle et al., *Scotland's Economy: Claiming the Future*, London: Verso, 1989, p. 5.

15. S. Kendrick, 'Social Change in Scotland', in G. Brown and R. Cook (eds), *Scotland: The Real Divide*, Edinburgh: Mainstream Publishing, 1989, p. 44.

16. G. McCrone, *Scotland's Future: The Economics of Nationalism*, Oxford: Blackwell, 1969, p. 7.

17. Boyle et al, *Scotland's Economy*, pp. 8–9.

18. McCrone, *Scotland's Future*, p. 35.

19. D. Newlands, 'The Regional Economies of Scotland', in T. Devine et al. (eds), *The Transformation of Scotland*, Edinburgh: Edinburgh University Press, 2005, p. 175.

20. N. Davidson, 'Neoliberal Politics in Devolved Scotland', in N. Davidson et al. (eds), *Neoliberal Scotland*, Cambridge: Cambridge Scholars Press, 2011, p. 318.

21. R. Leonard, 'Who Owns Scotland? The Reality of Economic Power', in P. Bryan (ed.) *People Power: The Labour Movement Alternative for Radical Constitutional Change*, Glasgow: Clydeside Press, 2012, p. 10.

22. C. Donald, 'Interdependence the Focus of City's Assembly', *The Scotsman*, 30 September 2006.

23. Quoted in C. Collins, '"The Scottish Executive is open for business": People and Place, The Royal Bank of Scotland, and the intensification of the neoliberal agenda in Scotland', in A. Cumbers and G. Whittam (eds), *Reclaiming the Scottish Economy*, Biggar: Scottish Left Review Press, 2007, p. 158.

24. G. Monbiot, 'The Cold Claims Lives While Energy Companies Get Rich', *Guardian*, 27 December 2010.

25. D. Miller, 'Profits and Parliament', *Scottish Left Review*, 24 (September–October 2004), p.. 15.

26. A. Law and G. Mooney, 'Urban Landscapes', *International Socialism*, Vol. 106 (Spring 2005).

27. G. Helms and A. Cumbers, 'Regulating the New Urban Poor: Local Labour Market Control in an Old Industrial City', paper presented at Work, Employment and Society Conference, Manchester, 1–3 September 2004.

28. Oxfam, 'Our Economy: Towards a New Prosperity', 2013, p. 14.

29. G. MacLeod, 'From Urban Entrepreneurialism to a 'Revanchist City'? On the Spatial Injustices of Glasgow's Renaissance', *Antipode*, Vol. 34, No. 3 (July 2002), pp. 602–24.

30. Oxfam, 'Our Economy: Towards a New Prosperity', p. 14.

31. T. Crichton, 'Child Poverty Scandal Costs £2 Billion a Year', *Daily Record*, 19 July 2013.

32. 'A Third of City Kids Live in Poverty', *Evening Times*, 18 February 2013.

33. I. Bell, 'Why Lessons Must Be Learned from this Catastrophic Failure', *The Herald*, 23 July 2011.

34. G. Monbiot, 'A Scandal of Secrecy and Collusion', *Guardian*, 28 December 2004.

35. V. Lambert, 'The Pros and Cons of PFI Hospitals', *Telegraph*, 10 March 2010.

36. Ibid.

37. A. Morris, 'Exclusive: We'll Pay £1.2bn for PFI Hospital But NEVER Own It', *Edinburgh Evening News*, 21 July 2010.

38. S. Carrell, 'NHS Board Consults Lawyers Over PFI Contract After Surgery Blackout', *Guardian*, 20 April 2012.

39. House of Commons Committee of Public Accounts, 'Lessons From PFI and Other Projects', Forty-fourth Report of Session 2010–12, London: TSO, 18 July 2011.

40. House of Commons Treasury Committee, 'Private Finance Initiative', Seventeenth Report of Session 2010–12, London: TSO, 18 July 2011, p. 3.

41. 'McConnell to Urge Scottish Labour to Embrace Enterprise', *Scotsman*, 27 February 2004.

42. D. Nelson and B. Laurance, 'Exposed: Lobbygate Comes to Scotland', *Observer*, 26 September 1999.

43. A. Law, 'Welfare Nationalism: Social Justice and/or Entrepreneurial Scotland?', in G. Mooney and G. Scott (eds), *Exploring Social Policy in the 'New' Scotland*, Bristol: Policy Press, 2005, p. 70.

44. 'Record View: Liar Lies Low', *Daily Record*, 28 October 1999.

45. K. Tribe, 'Liberalism and Neoliberalism in Britain, 1930–1980', in P. Mirowski and D. Plehwe (eds), *The Road from Mont Pelerin*, Cambridge: Harvard University Press, 2009, p. 90.

46. J. Scott and M. Hughes, 'Finance Capital and the Upper Classes', in G. Brown (ed.), *The Red Paper on Scotland*, Edinburgh: EUSPB, 1975, p. 184.

Chapter 4   Alliances and Divisions: Scottish Politics in the Holyrood Era

1. 'We've Never Had it So Good', *Scotsman*, 14 May 2004.

2. L. Paterson, F. Bechhofer and D. McCrone, *Living in Scotland*, Edinburgh: Edinburgh University Press, 2004, p. 80.

3. S. Payne, 'Not Even Conservative MPs Want to Attend Their Own Party Conference', *Spectator*, 13 September 2013.

4. S. Lansley, 'Life in the Middle: The Untold Story of Britain's Average Earners', Touchstone Pamphlet 6, TUC, 2009.

5. A. Law and G. Mooney, 'Financialisation and Proletarianisation: Changing Landscapes of Neoliberal Scotland', in N. Davidson et al. (eds), *Neoliberal Scotland*, Cambridge: Cambridge Scholars Press, p. 139.

6. J. Curtice, 'Elections and Public Opinion', in A. Seldon (ed.), *Blair's Britain*, Cambridge: Cambridge University Press, 2007, p. 42.

7. S. Watkins, 'A Weightless Hegemony', *New Left Review*, II/25, (January–February 2004), p. 6.

8. G. Hassan and E. Shaw, *The Strange Death of Labour Scotland*, Edinburgh: Edinburgh University Press, 2012, p. 88.

9. Ibid., p. 76.
10. Ibid.
11. R. Tait, 'Hard Left Threat to Dewar at Holyrood', *Scotsman*, 27 February 1999.
12. L. McGarvie, 'Cathy's Law', *Sunday Mail*, 25 May 2003.
13. M. Smith, 'Tracksuit Ambassadors', *Daily Mirror*, 6 June 2003.
14. Scottish Executive, 'Putting Our Communities First: A Strategy for Tackling Anti-social Behaviour', Consultation Paper on Tackling Anti-social Behaviour, 26 June 2003.
15. D. Fraser, 'Leader Steps to Left for Battle of "Nationalist Versus Socialist"', *Herald Scotland*, 31 March 2008.
16. A. Crawford, 'Socialism – the Answer to Scotland's Woes?', *Sunday Herald*, 23 June 2002.
17. M. Burns, 'A Red Paper Rescue for Lamont's Train Wreck', *Morning Star*, 1 October 2012.
18. R. Leonard, 'Labour's Need for a New Vision', *Morning Star*, 30 May 2011.
19. E. Barnes, 'Competence Not Constitution Won it for SNP', *Scotsman*, 22 June 2011.
20. W.L. Miller, 'The Death of Unionism?', in T.M. Devine (ed.), *Scotland and the Union 1707–2007*, Edinburgh: Edinburgh University Press, 2008, p. 188.
21. J. Mitchell, L. Bennie and R. Johns, *The Scottish National Party: Transition to Power*, Oxford: Oxford University Press, 2012, p. 64.
22. Ibid., p. 64.
23. Ibid., p. 62.
24. Ibid., p. 63.
25. Ibid., p. 125.
26. P. Surridge, 'The Scottish Electorate and Labour' in G. Hassan (ed.), *The Scottish Labour Party: History, Institutions and Ideas*, Edinburgh: Edinburgh University Press, 2004, p. 81.
27. M. Rosie and R. Bond, 'Social Democratic Scotland?', in M. Keating (ed.), *Scottish Social Democracy: Progressive Ideas for Public Policy*, Brussels: Peter Lang, 2007, p. 50.
28. A. Hussain and W. Miller, *Multicultural Nationalism: Islamophobia, Anglophobia, and Devolution*, Oxford: Oxford University Press, 2006, p. 33.
29. D. MacLeod and M. Russell, *Grasping the Thistle: How Scotland Must React to the Three Key Challenges of the Twenty First Century*, Glendaruel: Argyle Publishing, 2006.
30. M. Gray, '"Dirty Money?" The Tory Millionaire Bankrolling Better Together', *National Collective* [online], 7 April 2013 <http://nationalcollective.com/2013/04/07/dirty-money-the-tory-millionaire-bankrolling-better-together/>.
31. 'Swiss firm Vitol pleads guilty in UN oil/food case', *Reuters*, 20 November 2007.
32. E. Gosden, 'Vitol faces questions on trade with Iran', *Telegraph* , 26 September 2012.

33. R. Dinwoodie, 'No campaign urged to hand back money from oil chief', *Herald Scotland*, 11 April 2013.

34. Gray, '"Dirty Money?"'.

Chapter 5   Yes We Can, But We Need to Change: Strategy and 2014

1. P. Ramand and J. Foley, 'A Winning Strategy for Independence?', *Bella Caledonia* [online], 2012 <http://bellacaledonia.org.uk/2012/05/27/a-winning-strategy-for-independence/>.

2. L. Riddoch, 'The Yes Men', *Bella Caledonia* [online], 2012 <http://bellacaledonia.org.uk/2012/05/25/the-yes-men/>.

3. D. Torrance, *Salmond: Against the Odds*, Edinburgh: Birlinn, 2011, p. 6.

4. J. Curtice and R. Ormston, 'More Devolution: An Alternative Road? Evidence From Scottish Social Attitudes', *ScotCen Social Research*, 2012, p. 7.

5. 'Scottish Public Opinion Monitor: Scottish Government Approval Ratings', Ipsos MORI, 2013, p. 2.

6. Curtice and Ormston, 'More Devolution: An Alternative Road?', p. 10.

7. S. Johnson, 'Alex Salmond: Independent Scotland Will Remain Part of Five Unions', *Telegraph*, 13 July 2013.

8. Ibid.

9. G. Hassan, 'The Twilight of the British State: Alex Salmond, Scottish Independence and the European Question', *Open Democracy* [online], 28 October 2011 <http://www.gerryhassan.com/long-journalistic-essays/2020/>.

10. For example, T. Peterkin, 'Scottish independence: Theresa May Warns of Terror Threat After UK Split', *Scotsman*, 25 March 2012.

11. S. Noon, 'Why Positive Beats Negative', *SNmr* [online], 6 February 2011 <http://stephennoon.blogspot.co.uk/2011/02/why-positive-beats-negative.html>.

12. P. Ramand, 'Campaigning Strategies: Obama vs the SNP', *Bella Caledonia* [online], 6 November 2012 <http://bellacaledonia.org.uk/2012/11/06/campaigning-strategies-obama-v-the-snp/>.

13. Noon, 'Why Positive Beats Negative'.

14. S. Noon in Torrance, *Salmond: Against the Odds*, p. 7.

15. M. Rosie, and R. Bond, 'Social Democratic Scotland?' in M. Keating (ed.), *Scottish Social Democracy: Progressive Ideas for Public Policy*, Oxford: P.I.E. Peter Lang, 2007, pp. 39–57; G. Gall, *The Political Economy of Scotland: Red Scotland? Radical Scotland?*, Cardiff: University of Wales, 2005, pp. 67–84.

16 'Trident Jobs and Scotland's Economy', Scottish Campaign for Nuclear Disarmament report, 2010.

17. C. Harvie, *Fool's Gold: The Story of North Sea Oil*, London: Penguin, 1995, pp. 286–309 and 358–9.

18. B. Ehrenreich, *Bright-Sided: How Positive Thinking Is Undermining America*, New York: Metropolitan Books, 2009.

19. C. Craig, *The Tears that Made the Clyde: Well Being in Glasgow*, Glendaruel: Argyll Publishing, 2010.

20. W. Rennie, 'Scots Are Great. Independence Will Not Help Us to be Greater', *The Times*, 15 July 2013.

21. T. Gordon, 'Fear Versus Hope ... What History Tells Us', *Sunday Herald*, 7 July 2013.

22. A. Grice, 'Role in Iraq War "Has Made Britain a Target for Attacks"', *Independent*, 18 July 2005.

23. F. Gregory and P. Wilkinson, 'Riding Pillion for Tackling Terrorism is a High-risk Policy', in C. Browning and P. Cornish (eds), *Security, Terrorism and the UK*, ISP/NSC Briefing Paper 05/01 July 2005, New Security Challenges.

24. J. Curtice, 'Who Supports and Opposes Independence – and Why?', *ScotCen* [online], 15 May 2013 <http://www.scotcen.org.uk/media/1106700/who%20 supports%20and%20opposes%20independence%20and%20why.pdf>.

25. J. Maxwell, "The Scottish Yes campaign's Class Problem', *New Statesman*, 16 July 2012.

26. 'Four in Ten Scots Back Independence', Ipsos MORI [online], January 2012 <http://www.ipsos-mori.com/researchpublications/researcharchive/2912/ Four-in-ten-Scots-back-independence.aspx>.

27. J. Maxwell, 'To Recover, the Scottish Yes Campaign Needs to Go on the Attack', *New Statesman*, 24 January 2013.

Chapter 6   Scotland vs the Twenty-first Century: Towards a Radical Needs Agenda

1. R. Wilkinson and K. Pickett, *The Spirit Level: Why Equality is Better for Everyone*, London: Penguin, 2010, p. 224.

2. M. Fisher, *Capitalist Realism: Is There No Alternative?*, Ropley: Zero Books, 2009, p. 2.

3. K. Marx, *Critique of Hegel's Philosophy of Right*, Chicago: Aristeus, 2012, p. 9.

4. Scottish Government, 'Executive Summary', *The Government Economic Strategy – Part Two*, 2011.

5. P. Toynbee, *Hard Work: Life in Low-Pay Britain*, London: Bloomsbury, 2003, p. 6.

6. A. Park et al., 'British Social Attitudes, the 20th Report: Continuity and Change Over Two Decades', *NatCen*, London: Sage, 2003, p. 75.

7. Ibid.

8. M. Meacher, 'Wealth is Gushing Up in Britain, Not Trickling Down', *Sunday Telegraph*, 24 December 2006.

9. S. Milne, 'Ministers Now Accept the Gap Between Rich and Poor is Too Wide, But Still Refuse to Face the Political Cost of Action to Narrow It', *Guardian*, 16 August 2007.

10. 'High Earners, 2010 and 2011 Data', European Banking Authority [online], 15 July 2013 <http://www.eba.europa.eu/documents/10180/16145/EBA-Report-High_Earner_results.pdf>.

11. K. Trebeck and F. Stuart, 'Our Economy: Towards a New Prosperity', *Oxfam*, 20 June 2013.

12. R. Murphy, 'Why Are They Increasing the Tax Gap?', Public and Commercial Services Union, 2012.

13. Trebeck and Stuart, 'Our Economy: Towards a New Prosperity'.

14. H. Aldridge, P. Kenway and T. MacInnes, 'Monitoring Poverty and Social Exclusion in Scotland 2013', Joseph Rowntree Foundation, 2013.

15. R. Savio, 'Income Inequality to Reach Victorian-Era Levels by 2025', Inter Press Service, 12 September 2013.

16. G. Monbiot, 'An 87% Cut by 2030', *Guardian*, 21 September 2006.

17. 'Capitalising the Green Investment Bank: Key issues and next steps', Ernst and Young, October 2010.

18. D. Sharma, 'Most Fuel Subsidies Are Being Doled Out in the Rich West', *Morning Star*, 4 December 2012.

19. J. Vidal, 'Rapid Arctic Thawing Could be Economic Timebomb, Scientists Say', *Guardian*, 5 July 2013.

20. P. Inman, 'Billionaires' Fortunes Hinder Fight Against Poverty, Says Oxfam', *Guardian*, 19 January 2013.

21. N. Klein, 'How Science is Telling us all to Revolt', *New Statesman*, 29 October 2013.

22. T.H. Marshall, *Citizenship and Social Class*, London: Pluto Press, 1997.

23. E.O. Wright, *Envisioning Real Utopias*, London: Verso, 2010, p. 115.

24. N. Davidson, 'Neoliberal Politics in a Devolved Scotland', in N. Davidson, P. McCafferty and D. Miller (eds), *Neoliberal Scotland: Class and Society in a Stateless Nation*, Newcastle: Cambridge Scholars, 2010.

25. 'Not By the People: The Launch of the Commission on Fair Access to Political Influence', Jimmy Reid Foundation, 3 February 2013.

26. E.O. Wright, *Envisioning Real Utopias*, London: Verso, 2010, pp. 117–19; B. Ackerman, *Voting with Dollars: a New Paradigm for Campaign Finance*, New Haven, CT: Yale University Press, 2004.

27. 'Priced Out', Research and Media Department, Barnardo's [online], February 2012 <http://www.barnardos.org.uk/pricedoutreport.pdf>.

28. L. Elliot et al., 'A Green New Deal: Joined-up Policies to Solve the Triple Crunch of the Credit Crisis, Climate Change and High Oil Prices', Green New Deal Group [online], 2008 <http://www.neweconomics.org/publications/entry/a-green-new-deal>.

29. A. Whiteman, 'Land Reform and Land Restitution in Post-Feudal Scotland', Paper presented at 'Squatters or Settlers: Rethinking Ownership, Occupation and Use in Land Law' conference, International Institute for the Sociology of Law, Euskadi, 1–3 June 2005.

30. J. Brown, 'Imagine a Feudal Country Where 432 Families Own Half the Land. Welcome to Scotland', *Independent*, 2 August 2013.

31. 'Danish Tycoon is Owner of Scotland', *Sunday Mail*, 7 July 2013.

32. T. Crichton, 'Greediest Benefit Claimants in Scotland: Legal Loopholes of the Rich and Famous', *Daily Record*, 12 July 2013.

33. G. Monbiot, 'Windfarms are Stricken by the British Refusal to Share', *Guardian*, 25 March 2010.

34. P. Kingsley, 'Windfarms: Is Community Ownership the Way Ahead?', *Guardian*, 6 November 2012.

35. H. Corcoran and D. Wilson, 'The Worker Co-operative Movements in Italy, Mondragon and France: Context, Success Factors and Lessons', Canadian Worker Co-operative Federation, May 2010.

36. In October 2013, workers at the Ineos-owned oil refinery and petrochemical plant in Grangemouth announced strike action after the victimisation of a union official. Billionaire owner Jim Ratcliffe threatened to close down the petrochemical plant and walk away, leaving workers facing the sack. The threat was withdrawn after they agreed to humiliating concessions, including a three-year pay freeze, pensions downgrading, and an anti-union clause covering the next three years.

37. See R. Blackburn, *Age Shock*, London: Verso, 2011, p. 158.

38. J. Glennie, 'Cuba: A Development Model that Proved the Doubters Wrong', *Guardian*, 5 August 2011.

39. This idea was developed by L. Elliot et al., 'A Green New Deal: Joined-up policies to solve the triple crunch of the credit crisis, climate change and high oil prices', Green New Deal Group [online], 2008 <http://www.neweconomics.org/publications/entry/a-green-new-deal>.

40. R. Blake, 'North Sea Oil: It's Not Whether There's Going to be a "Boom" but Who Owns it that Matters', Radical Independence [online], 18 March 2013 <http://radicalindependence.org/index.php/2013/03/18/north-sea-oil-its-not-whether-theres-going-to-be-a-boom-but-who-owns-it-that-matters/>.

41. For more on this, see J. Cuthbert and M. Cuthbert, 'Economic Policy Options for an Independent Scotland', Jimmy Reid Foundation, September 2013, pp. 6–12.

42. R. Blackburn, 'A Global Pension', *New Left Review*, Vol. 47 (September–October 2007); J. Stiglitz, *Globalisation and its Discontents*, London: Penguin, 2002.

43. M. Danson, J. MacFarlane and W. Sullivan, 'Investing in the Good Society: Five Questions on Tax and the Common Weal', Jimmy Reid Foundation, September 2013.

44. A. Bowman et al., 'The Great Train Robbery: Rail Privatisation and After', Centre for Research on Socio-Cultural Change, June 2013.

45. 'Thrive at Five: Comparative Child Development at School Entry Age', Save the Children, Edinburgh: STC, 2012.

46. 'Analysis of Data From Higher Education Statistics Agency', Centre for Educational Sociology, 2013.

47. 'Thrive at Five'.

48. N. Grubb, H. Marit Jahr, J. Neumüller, S. Field, 'Equity in Education: Thematic Review', OECD [online], 21 April 2005 <http://www.oecd.org/education/innovation-education/36376641.pdf>.

49. J. Maxwell, 'The SNP Confronts its Defence Problem', *New Statesman*, 18 October 2012.

Afterword: After the White Paper, After Britain

1. K. McKenna, 'Alex Salmond Aims for Independence White Paper with a Literary Twist', *Observer*, 13 July 2013.

2. A. Massie, 'Ask not "Why" – but "Why Not?"', *The Times*, 27 November 2013.

3. B. Jamieson, 'White Paper Fails Examination', *Scotsman*, 27 November 2013.

4. K. Allen, 'Equal pay for women not likely till 2067, says research', *Guardian*, 19 August 2010.

5. I. MacWhirter, 'The nation's going south … and Scotland's paying for it', *Herald*, 14 November 2013.

6. M. Dailly, 'Inequalities of Fact', *Mike Dailly* [online], 27 November 2013.

7. 'Britain Most Unequal Nation in Europe', *Press TV* [online], 29 December 2012.

8. Ibid.

9. 'UK Wages Decline Among Worst in Europe', *BBC* [online], 11 August 2013.

10. 'UK Second in European Fuel Poverty League', *ITV* [online], 25 October 2013.

11. M. King, 'UK housing costs the third highest in Europe', *Guardian*, 19 July 2012.

12. M. Thompson, 'UK Petition for Fair Pensions – Neglect of the Elderly is a Disgrace', *Think Left* [online], 22 July 2013.

13. S. Cassidy, More than 1 in 5 British Pensioners at Risk of Poverty', *Independent*, 8 June 2012.

14. C. Cooper, 'UK Warned that Youth Unemployment is "Public Health Time Bomb Waiting to Explode"', *Independent*, 30 October 2013.

15. 'Research Digest #2 – Income Inequality: Trends and Measures', *The Equality Trust* [online], 5 July 2011.

16. Ibid.

17. T.H. Marshall, 'Citizenship and Social Class', in C. Pierson and F.G. Castles (eds), *The Welfare State Reader*, London: Polity Press, 2006, p. 38.

18. T. Gordon, 'One Year On: Will Better Together Change their Tactics?', *Herald*, 22 June 2013.

19. See B. Ehrenreich, *Bright-Sided: How the Relentless Promotion of Positive-Thinking has Undermined America*, New York: Metropolitan Books, 2009.

7660525R00085

Printed in Great Britain
by Amazon.co.uk, Ltd.,
Marston Gate.